THE
ART
OF
SPIRIT

THE ART OF SPIRIT

*The Most Enigmatic Paintings
And Drawings Ever Created*

ANN BRIDGE DAVIES

Ann Bridge Davies © 2020

All rights reserved
in accordance with the Copyright, Designs and Patents Act 1988.

No parts of this publication may be reproduced, stored in a retrieval system, or transmitted in any form or by any means whatsoever without the prior permission of the publisher.

A record of this publication is available from the British Library.

ISBN 978-1-910027-33-2

Typesetting by Wordzworth Ltd
www.wordzworth.com

Cover design by Titanium Design Ltd
www.titaniumdesign.co.uk

Cover image: *Pearl* by Mary and Elizabeth Bangs,
by kind permission of Dr Hans Ulrich Schär

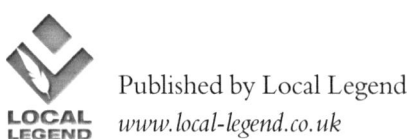

Published by Local Legend
www.local-legend.co.uk

GRATITUDE

Writing this book has been a challenge to me, both an agony and an ecstasy. Shortly after deciding to write it as an academic thesis, I was found to have a genetic illness that resulted in major hospital treatment, forcing me to give up the academic path as 'life' took over. Yet it is my life's purpose to bring this wonderful canon of little known art history into the light of public awareness, so I persevered.

I am deeply grateful to all the special people who have helped me on this long journey: those who helped with the writing, who made vital connections regarding where to find some of the more elusive forms of spirit art, those who gave me emotional and physical support and those artists who were part of the story and who have now returned home to Spirit.

Firstly, a great 'thank you' to Dorothy Davies, friend and reader who was by my side when I was on the point of binning the lot. She said, "This has to be written – and you are the only one to do it." I would also like to thank Susan Farrow for just being there, offering support in invisible ways.

On my American journey, I am indebted to many at the Lily Dale Assembly, especially Ron Nagy for sharing his tremendous knowledge of the special works there, to Susan Barnes for hosting me, to spirit artist Joe Sheil and to Mandy in the Lily Dale Library. I thank Lauren Thibodeau for opening my eyes in New York to the American spirit artworks, especially the portraits at Lily Dale, and New York writer and spirit photographer Shannon Taggard.

I also acknowledge my publisher Nigel Peace for his wisdom and editing, Vivienne Roberts of the College of Psychic Studies,

Paul Gaunt of the Arthur Findlay College, the staff of the Cambridge University Library Archive and the many living and working spirit artists, especially Alan Stuttle. My deepest thanks also go to the photographer Marianthi Lainas, whose work made many old images suitable for publication.

Last but not least, I give my gratitude to those who have remained with me through very trying times over many years, especially my husband Rod Davies, my friend Adrian Horn and my birthday buddy Paul Craig.

ACKNOWLEDGEMENTS

The publisher wishes to offer sincere gratitude to those who have given kind permission for artworks in their ownership or care to be reproduced here:

Curator Vivienne Roberts and Principal Gill Matini of the College of Psychic Studies, London, for Georgiana Houghton's *The Flower of Catherine Emily Stringer* and for Frank Leah's *Portrait of a Man*.

The Committee of the Portsmouth Temple of Spiritualism for the Bangs sisters' *Iola*.

Curator Paul Gaunt of the Britten Museum & Library, The Arthur Findlay College, Stansted Hall, Essex, and the Spiritualists' National Union, for David Duguid's two *Untitled* direct paintings.

The Society for Psychical Research and the Syndics of Cambridge University Library, for Anna Mary Howitt's *Untitled* (pencil drawing of boy), *Untitled* (watercolour) and *Untitled* (pencil drawing of woman and child).

Ms Susan B Barnes for José Medrado's *Ida* (after Renoir) and for her own work, *Egypt*.

Ms Erika Andreasson for her portrait of *Yngve*.

Ms Saleire Tracy for her portrait of *Julie*.

The Lily Dale Assembly, New York, for the Campbell brothers' *Azur the Helper* and *Nora* and for the Bangs sisters' *Clara*.

Mr Joe Shiel for *Woman*.

Ms Wendy Redfern for Coral Polge's *Grandmother* and *Spirit Guide*.

Mr Paul Clarke for his painting of *Alan*.

Mr Mark Foster for his Poly-Interference aura photograph.

Dr Hans Ulrich Schär for the Bangs sisters' *Pearl*.

Nigel Peace for John Cotton's *The Franciscan Guide*.

Other images are owned by the author or are in the public domain.

THE AUTHOR

Born in Liverpool, UK, Ann Bridge Davies found that she could communicate with the spirit world as a young child, but was labelled "evil" by her local priest. This caused her to turn away from spirituality and, instead, become a qualified Art teacher and practising artist.

Everything changed a few years later when she was told by a respected medium that, indeed, she was a 'spirit artist' with the ability to combine her natural talents in providing evidence of an afterlife. She then trained as a medium under the tutelage of the great Glyn Edwards, Gordon Higginson and Coral Polge (who acknowledged Ann as her 'successor'). And for the next thirty-five years she taught Art and created portraits of the so-called deceased across the UK, in the USA, throughout Europe and even in Dubai.

Realising that spirit art had never been recognised by the establishment (often referred to as 'Outsider Art'), Ann began academic research of its history and was the first to recognise that there is not just one form but six clear types of spirit art. In this fascinating and unique book, she describes the awe-inspiring drawings and paintings that have been manifested by the use of paranormal energies, often created without any human intervention. These artworks are like no others in the world and they challenge every one of us to rethink everything we thought we knew about human consciousness.

"This book," says Ann, "has been my life's work."

The Author's Previous Publications

Portraits from Spirit (AuthorHouse UK, 2011)

ABOUT THIS BOOK

From the mid-nineteenth century to the present day, a handful of dedicated, humble artists and mediums have been producing the most extraordinary and beautiful work, from visionary images to evidential portraiture, that seeks to prove the existence of an afterlife.

These enigmatic paintings and drawings have largely been ignored by an uncomprehending art establishment – until now, when they are being recognised as both an important genre deserving of major exhibitions and a vital contribution to the understanding of human consciousness.

This is a unique and authoritative history that focuses on the major contributors, written from the artists' point of view by a practising spirit artist.

CONTENTS

Foreword   xv

Introduction   1

PART ONE
Experimental Mediumship
Mediumistic Automatism and Trance Art   **9**

Chapter 1   Nineteenth Century Automatism and Figurative Art   17

Chapter 2   Nineteenth Century Automatism and Abstraction   37

Chapter 3   Late Nineteenth Century Trance Art   55

PART TWO
Physical Mediumship
Portrait and Figurative Painting   **75**

Chapter 4   Psychographic Art, Slate Writing and Portraiture   81

Chapter 5   Precipitated Portrait Painting   99

Chapter 6   Precipitated Portrait and Figure Painting   115

PART THREE
Mental Mediumship
Modern Evidential Spirit Portraiture and Contemporary Spirit Art   **127**

Chapter 7	Mid-Twentieth Century Evidential Portrait Drawing	133
Chapter 8	Late Twentieth Century Evidential Drawing	147
Chapter 9	Contemporary Spirit Art	159
Reflections		187
Bibliography		193

FOREWORD

Professor John Harvey,
BA (CNAA) MA (Wales) PhD (Wales) FRSA

This book is the first to survey a dimension of paranormal phenomena that, hitherto, has not received the attention it deserves. Whether or not you affirm the underlying supernatural presuppositions, "this most unusual history" (as the author rightly refers to it) will fascinate and beguile.

Ann Bridge Davies provides an accessible account of the spirit art tradition – and it is no less than that. Key concepts are clearly explained and a background adequate to the topic's discussion provided. She also helpfully charts the chronological development of the tradition whilst, at the same time, constructing a taxonomy of its varied manifestations.

This is an art of amanuensis in which the process of manufacture is often more sublimely intriguing than the product. The latter serves as the relic and proof of an interaction between the material world and an immaterial agency – as well as of the survival of consciousness and creativity after death.

It is a tradition within which Ann has sought to situate herself as a practitioner. In so doing, she offers a rare insider's perspective, one that is balanced and insightful. The author is not blind to the possibility of either fraudulence or self-delusion on the part of some mediums or to the credulity of an audience that was too eager to believe. But nor does she dismiss the notion that what may appear to be unlikely and inexplicable is, therefore, necessarily unreal and untrue.

Whatever else you conclude after reading Ann's book, you'll not doubt her passionate advocacy, which has been born of a conviction informed by personal experience.

John Harvey
Professor of Art,
Aberystwyth University

INTRODUCTION

Frank Leah was an artist for whom, as the spiritualist writer and historian Maurice Barbanell would say, "The dead pose in his studio." He used his talents of clairvoyance and artistry to draw thousands of portraits of deceased people, which were then identified by relatives or friends of the subjects. Many believe that these images offer proof of our survival after physical death.

Inspired by Leah, and as a working artist myself, I decided to study and create this form of art in my own practice. Exploring its history and delving into how and why the pioneers created their art, I realised that the early paintings and drawings were mainly experimental. But they were never really accepted by the art world at that time, the mid-1800s, despite mainstream art undergoing radical change. The reason for this was possibly less to do with the quality of the work and more that it was underpinned by two beliefs: that the human being survives death and is known as a spirit, and that the spirit is able to communicate with the living.

It is generally accepted that the new religion of Spiritualism was inaugurated on the 31st March, 1848, in Hydesville, New York State, in a wooden cottage belonging to the Fox family. A belief in spirits and ghosts has been common, of course, in many cultures since human life began, but now a series of paranormal events caused an entire township to take notice. A deceased man, who identified himself, seemed to be persistently attempting to communicate by rapping on the wooden walls of the cottage. The raps spelled out, in a form of Morse code, that he had been murdered and that he wanted justice!

The Hydesville events were widely publicised and brought many to believe in human survival of death and, moreover, that spirits in 'the afterlife' deserved respect. From this grew the religious practice of Spiritualism along with serious investigation of these and similar paranormal events.[1] In particular, there was a focus on the medium, the one communicating between the worlds of the living and the dead. This principle of communication suggests a symbiotic relationship between spirit and medium and, from this belief structure, art has evolved as one form of conduit.

The supernatural activities associated with 'spirit contact' do not only take the form of rappings but also other physical phenomena such as teleportation (the movement of objects without human involvement), translocation (the movement of objects through solid walls, for example) and materialisation (the apparent creation of objects, including spirit forms, often said to be by means of a substance called ectoplasm). The creation of spirit art also seems to require these processes, together with drawing and painting skills.

Of course, not everyone believes the 'truth' of Spiritualism and its essential philosophy of the continuous existence of the human soul, which has never been scientifically proven (and possibly never could be). And whilst virtually all religions believe in the existence of an afterlife in some form or other, there is no other faith where the deceased appear able to create paintings and drawings. For this reason, and for this study, the principles of Spiritualism have to be taken as the basis for classifying the different forms of paranormal artistic expression. It is not for us here to query life-after-death theories but to explore the art as it has been created through the practices of those who *have* believed and spent their lives creating art by their beliefs.

---

[1] Twenty years later, Spiritualism's religious principles were first defined. Spiritualism is now a recognised religion in both the USA and the UK.

INTRODUCTION

The first such art was the work of an American minister, John Murray Spear (1804-1887), in 1852. Then two Victorian female artists in particular, Georgiana Houghton (1814-1884) and Anna Mary Howitt (1824-1884), took up the challenge and began to create spirit paintings too. But British Victorian mainstream art, which the women attempted to enter, was dominated in the mid-nineteenth century by the critical views of John Ruskin (1819-1900) who did not support any art, or artist, using a method that was not fully understood. Ruskin, a powerful critic, shunned the experimental work of artist-mediums thus delaying its progress considerably.

This book is therefore both a history of art and of the trials, troubles and joys of mediums and artists, trained and untrained alike, who followed their religious convictions to the very end. They fully believed that they were allowing spirits to draw through them, to possess them or to conjoin energies with them in order to create art. Most of these men and women suffered socially for their belief that a human consciousness, after death of the physical body, could draw and paint from a spirit world. They produced abstract images, portraits, landscapes, familial scenes and religious artefacts for little or no money and certainly no accolade, believing that they were doing good for mankind.

Their art forms had little value outside their religion. Moreover, as an art lecturer for over forty-five years, I found that whilst other canons of religious art have an explicit place in the structure of art history, 'Spirit Art' is not even mentioned. This led me to try to discover why this should be, ultimately realising that artwork created under the philosophical conditions of spiritualistic praxis were looked upon, by the art establishment, as nonsense and discredited because supernatural phenomena are largely misunderstood. Yet this culture is immensely rich both in its subject matter and means of production.

However the work is classified – there are different forms being produced differently – there is one shared aim and the end product is a genuinely unique canon of art. The supernatural techniques create the procedure, the artist's beliefs bring the inspiration and the paranormal energies form the adhesive to bind the image together. The spirit, the artist and the recipient of the art become one thread in the making of a visual message from the believed immaterial world. And the medium-as-artist reaches out to the observer, attempting to recreate a form of *genius loci* – the personal atmosphere or presence of a spirit – as the recipients of the work watch and wait in order to identify with the subject.

What, then, is this 'spirit' that the artist is attempting to capture? Reflecting upon what makes up a person's presence, the philosopher, artist and writer David Crouch remarked drily, "In life some people are lifeless, so what are they in spirit?" In the philosophy of Spiritualism, the spirit is understood to be an 'ethereal' person, yet still holding the memories and personality of the once-living, which mediums can sense (whether by feeling, hearing or seeing). The character of the deceased has not changed with death and it is this individuality that helps identify the spirit; in virtually every case, the medium would not have met him or her in life.

But while working as a mediumistic artist myself for over thirty years, even I was not aware that there were types of spirit art other than 'evidential portraits'. Twelve years of study led me to the conclusion that there is not just one classification for 'art of the spirit' but six different types, determined by the techniques used in making them. Further, I discovered that these groups of artworks have several forms in their creation. I have named these classifications as:

1. Mediumistic Automatism
2. Trance Art
3. Psychographic Art
4. Precipitated Art
5. Modern Evidential Spirit Art
6. Contemporary Spirit Art

INTRODUCTION

As I studied the art, spoke with owners and curators and visited the homes, galleries, churches and centres where the various types of work were housed, it became clear that whilst the nineteenth century art was generally already named, later work needed to be entitled differently. I also realised that titles of known pieces explained the processes by which the art was made. For example, Mediumistic Automatism reflected the automatic movements of the medium during the creative process and Trance Art was produced when the artist was in that state.

The techniques for creating Mediumistic Automatism appeared similar, I felt, to those of Surrealist Automatism so it was helpful to find this comment by the artist André Breton (1896-1966): "I consider the hypothesis of 'spirits' to be ridiculous and, more generally, I dissociate myself *a priori* from all spiritualist interpretation of hypnotic phenomena."[2] For the sake of his own genre, Breton here defines the two art forms as being absolutely different. Although he seems to have been repulsed by spirit art, his exclamation is helpful for this study because it distinguishes between the two genres and confirms that spirit art needs to be looked upon as a separate art form.

While organising the sections for this book, I wondered how to set the scene for this most unusual history. Firstly, the methods by which the art has been created (the classifications above) are themselves unique, not just the typical processes used in the making of any art. But then there is also the supernatural aspect, which can be divided into three parts:

1. The early experimental mediumship mentioned already;
2. Physical mediumship; and
3. Mental mediumship resulting in evidential art.

---

[2] *André Breton and the First Principles of Surrealism* (Franklin Rosemont, Pluto Press, 1987)

Thus the chapters have been organised both chronologically and by types of mediumship, focusing on artists who used different psychic and artistic processes. We begin from 1852, with Mediumistic Automatism and Trance Art within experimental mediumship's Part One; Psychographic Art and Precipitated Painting have their place within Part Two, relating to physical mediumship; finally we have Evidential Art and Contemporary Art in Part Three, as mental mediumship.

These three Parts were created in order to differentiate between the supernatural processes so that the forms of art could also be shown to be completely different. The supernatural methods are explained alongside the art techniques and independent artist biographies, revealing the flow of the work as a historical document.

My information was acquired in three ways: by visiting the places where the art is kept and interviewing its curators, by reading about those who personally viewed the art as it was created (in the case of now deceased artists) and by speaking to the artists themselves (for the contemporary section).

There have been several exhibitions of spirit artwork in England, which was helpful in gaining more insight into the work of Georgiana Houghton. Her works and those of Anna Mary Howitt were referred to in Rachel Oberter's PhD thesis[3], which led me to the Cambridge University Library where some wonderful examples of Howitt's work are stored. Friends found books for me that were difficult to locate, such as the Howitt family biography and the story of *Pearl*. Few texts exist regarding Psychographic and Precipitated Art, though, which was why case studies have been used together with interviews with Ron Nagy, curator of the Lily Dale Assembly Museum. For the Contemporary Art, the owners of works and the artists who made them were very willing to give their accounts and to share photographs.

---

[3] *Spiritualism and the Visual Imagination in Victorian Britain* (Rachel Oberter, Yale University, 2007)

INTRODUCTION

Given that spirit art has never before been classified or catalogued, I feel sure that this study is only the beginning and that there is much more to discover and to learn about the manner in which apparently quite ordinary people turn, for example, to drawing portraits of deceased individuals whom they have never met, while also describing the histories of their subjects. The artist-mediums have faith that what they are doing, for little or no financial reward, is helping another person understand spiritual principles.

However, it is evident from the lack of representation of the work described in this book in conventional art history, or even that of religious art, that these paintings and drawings are anomalies, little known or understood. For the most part, they seem to have been hidden within the spiritualist religion and unexamined, resting undetected in cupboard drawers, rarely framed or exhibited, remaining unspoken of in art culture. They deserve to be recognised as works of art in their own right.

PART ONE

EXPERIMENTAL MEDIUMSHIP

Mediumistic Automatism and Trance Art

FOREWORD

From the inception of Spiritualism, those who saw, felt or heard communications from the spirit world experimented with supernatural energies in their dark séances, thus generating the first type of spirit art. These pioneers were highly creative artist-mediums who were willing for the 'forces' to work through them, producing paintings and drawings created by allowing the physical body to succumb to spirit control. This resulted in a form of automatic mark-making, using the mediumistic techniques of automatism and trance, which in the mid-nineteenth century was a unique creative process both in terms of art and spiritualistic method.

There are written testimonies about some of those working in this way at that time. The first such artist was John Murray Spear (1804-1887) who began to draw as spirit controlled him.

"In May 1852, his hand was seized with the compulsion to draw. He said he had 'never had any taste for drawing' and 'never drew the first thing in his life', but he gave his hand a pen to work its will. His hand drew a picture of itself, and then other parts of his body, and then labelled the pictures with diagrams, emblems and mottoes: 'open thine hand to the poor' was written in the palm of his hand… The spirits were preparing him for a new mission… Soon he began other spontaneous, abstract and automatic drawings, very singular and sometimes beautiful diagrams of things which he and no-one else on Earth… ever saw or heard of before."[4]

---

[4] *The Remarkable Life of John Murray Spear* (J B Buescher, University of Notre Dame Press, 2006)

John Spear was probably not aware of his own achievement at the time but, by putting a graphite pencil in his hand and "asking for God's guidance", his experimental action began a new movement in both art and mediumship. Beginning by simply letting his hand move and to be taken over by an impulse that he believed was from a spirit, within a few seconds he created drawings from what he believed to be God's messengers, the angels of the spirit world. This action defined the future of spirit art.

After the Hydesville events of 1848, séances had become rife. The news of ghostly rappings from a deceased pedlar soon spread from America to Britain and on to Europe, stirring people to sit in their parlours waiting for communication from the dead. From the American homesteads came exciting tales not only of noises from the wooden walls of the cottages, but of chairs and pianos flying around sitting rooms! Even President Abraham Lincoln and his wife became involved in séances, suggesting that such paranormal events should be taken seriously. Then, through experimentation with the artist's tools of pencil and paper alongside supernatural energies, the movement of spirit art began.

Considering these drawings as quasi-religious manifestations of God's hand through His spirit helpers, John Spear's example of allowing the hand to move independently from the mind influenced early protagonists of Spiritualism in England, furthering the movement throughout Great Britain. Here, others among the first to create drawings without conscious thought were the Quakers William Martin Wilkinson (1814-1897) and his wife Elizabeth. There were also the Plain Quakers William Howitt (1792-1879) and his wife Mary (1799-1888), who were writers to the Victorian court. Their daughter Anna Mary Howitt (1824-1884), who would prove to be one of the great pioneers of spirit art, described these beginnings in *Pioneers of Spiritual Reformation* (1883):

"One Sunday, January 31st, 1858, my father much to his astonishment gained the power to write, and also to draw. He and my mother a day or two previously had visited Mr and Mrs W

Wilkinson at Hampstead to inspect the remarkable and beautiful spirit-given drawings of Mr Wilkinson, the origin and production of which caused Mr Wilkinson to publish his valuable book…"[5]

Anna Mary also described her experience at a séance held in 1872, of how William Wilkinson had created his first spirit art:

"The influence [of spirit] becoming stronger and ever stronger, moved not alone the hand but the whole arm in a rotary motion until the arm was at length raised and rapidly – as if it had been the spoke of a wheel propelled by machinery – whirled irresistibly in a whole sweep, and with great speed, for some ten minutes through the air. The effect of this rapid rotation was felt by him in the muscles of the arm for some little time afterwards." (*Spirit Identity*, Appendix, 1872.)

These passages are invaluable for understanding the manner and process by which spirit art was first created. The hand seemed to be held in a tight grip by the spirit; the arm rotated so fiercely that it could not be stopped by the person affected; and those influenced by the unseen spirit force did not try to stop the procedure, believing that they were being guided by the world of God and the departed.

Today, it would be thought that the discarnate spirit does not actually grip the hand of the artist but affects the part of the brain that causes involuntary movement of the arm and hand. But those first artists relied upon what they believed about how a spirit connects, communicates and physically uses their human body to write and draw. Each séance was a time of experimentation and investigation, as each would-be artist in their own way attempted to link with whomever (or whatever) wanted to use their physical body.

Spear was a pioneer and forerunner to the techniques future artists would use: the 'hand of spirit' finding a way to trigger the

---

[5] *Spirit Drawings: A Personal Narrative* (Wilkinson, W M, Chapman & Hall, 1858; reprinted by Trieste Publishing, 2018)

medium's brain into moving the hand, arm or whole body automatically. These mediums must have had a great deal of faith in what they were doing and creating, at a time – let it not be forgotten – when women were often placed in mental institutions for any form of odd behaviour. Women took the risk of being marked publicly with madness each time they visited a séance room and allowed themselves to be controlled by invisible forces who drew, wrote and spoke through those present.

Two women in particular independently facilitated and evolved spirit-inspired art as a tool for their religious belief and in the development of their artistic talent. From the mid-nineteenth century until 1884, the year they both died, Anna Mary Howitt (whose married name was Watts) and Georgiana Houghton dominated spirit art in England. Although they probably did not realise it at the time, they became the most significant of the Victorian spiritualists to explore both the supernatural, through paranormal experiments, and the art techniques they had learned in their education. They used spirit energies and art materials to create paintings and drawings, their supernatural methods requiring a conviction that they could achieve communication with the spirits of the dead, who controlled the artists' bodily movements as a form of automatism.

It is not known whether Anna Mary Howitt and Georgiana Houghton ever met but it is known through their separate writings[6] that they had similar convictions regarding communication with the deceased. These writings are important to the understanding of their art in that they give accounts of how the automated works were created. By explaining the concept that art could be created by spirit-mediums, in amanuensis to the spirits

---

[6] *Evenings at Home in Spiritual Séance: Welded Together by a Species of Autobiography* (Georgiana Houghton, Forgotten Books, 1882, reprinted Kessinger Pub, 2008) and *Pioneers of the Spiritual Reformation: Biographical Sketches* (Anna Mary Howitt, 1883, reprinted Cambridge University Press, 2011)

of the dead, their art became *a representation of the spirit world itself,* as experienced by the deceased. However, these supernatural convictions, although very real to Howitt and Houghton, placed the women and others who followed in a precarious social position at a time when women were fighting for their right to be accepted as equal to men.

Indeed, the new religious model of Spiritualism proposed equality between people, races and genders through the Principles of its faith. Thus, in theory, financial value should not have been an issue. But whilst Howitt's family were moderately well off as writers to the Victorian court, Houghton was financially indebted to patrons who took an interest in her spirit messages and pictures from the dead. In this way, Spiritualism was more than a religious pursuit. Yes, it offered some inner comfort to both the spirit-mediums and the recipients of the verbal and visual messages, but these artworks also provided an income to those who needed it. Anna Mary Howitt's texts regarding Spiritualism and its art illustrated valuable historical evidence of the reasons why she followed her path as a spiritualist artist rather than that of a conventional artist in her own right. But Georgiana Houghton's writing indicated that she developed her use of mediumistic automatism for another motive, that of financial security.

Anna Mary created small, simple but unfinished watercolour paintings and drawings that emerged from the darkened Victorian séances. There has to be a question as to why her spirit-influenced paintings and drawings lacked the aesthetic and very beautiful quality that her own academic art works possessed. The comparison between the two forms suggests that there may have been some unconscious interference between her artistry and her religious beliefs. Concerned about this, her mother, the writer Mary Howitt, thought her daughter "vulnerable"; although sympathetic to spiritualist values herself, she shared the Victorian supposition that the human mind could become "prey to psychic delusions which could become moribund."[7] Of course, this was the curse of sitting for night after night in dark and cold séance rooms for the sake of art.

This point regarding the difference between academic and spirit art work is important because we find a similar variance of aesthetic quality between an artist's personal work and their experimental spirit art throughout this history. Could this be because the artist believes that they are being led or controlled by spirits, accordingly they expect the works to be different in style and content? This is especially true of Georgiana Houghton's work.

In the world of contemporary art, she is referred to as an 'outsider artist' and was described as such at the 2016 exhibition of her work at the Courtauld Gallery in London. However, her paintings were created through her religious belief – during séance conditions, both light and dark, and are spiritualist in philosophical origin – and so should properly be known as spirit art. There was a lack of general contemporary awareness of this canon at the time, so her abstracted, highly-coloured and complicated linear artwork, with some qualities of outsider art, divided opinion. The classification was reinforced by the Prinzhorn Collection at the beginning of the twentieth century (the works of mentally ill patients) and by Charles Russell's book *Groundwaters: A Century of Art by Self-Taught and Outsider Artists*. Interestingly, Houghton did not have her work criticised as did Howitt, possibly because she was not so much an academically trained artist (and thus her work would supposedly be of no interest to the buying public at the time).

Out of the experimentation with spirit energies and art materials grew a second classification of spirit art, namely Trance Art. Scottish joiner David Duguid (1832-1907) was one of the first

---

[7] *The Darkened Room: Women, Power and Spiritualism in Late Victorian England* (Alex Owen, Oxford University Press, 2004)

such artists. Although his work is closely connected to the earlier form by the use of psychic processes, Duguid did not remain fully conscious during its creation, unlike Spear, Wilkinson, Howitt and Houghton. (His work and artistic method is fully explained in Chapter Three.)

By allowing the spirit world to work through them, their bodies controlled by paranormal forces, these mediumistic artists created the first two classifications of what we now term spirit art. There are many today (including healer and medium Matthew Manning) who still use these techniques of experimentation with automatism and trance in order to create artwork. The efforts of the Victorian mediums gave much to the future of the genre by their solid determination and courage.

1
Nineteenth Century Automatism and Figurative Art

Anna Mary Howitt was a key figure in the early stages of spirit art as she watched and carefully studied her father and his friends create their spirit-controlled drawings. There is little to see now of the early art by John Spear and William Howitt but Anna Mary, as an artist in her own right, kept small impressions of her spirit art which were bequeathed to Cambridge University, although left unclassified. We are fortunate to have these pieces of evidence since without them there would be little of her spiritual life and work to see. Her delicate watercolours, drawings and automatic writing give us some idea not only of how the spirit world worked with her as a mediumistic artist but also what the conjoining of Spirit and artist could do. Such artists had to believe that a form of life existed after death and be willing to give up their body and mind in order to surrender completely to one or more aspects of 'God, the angels and the deceased' as they made their art.

As well as this otherworldly input, Howitt required the support of her family in order to fulfil her spiritual and creative work, since talking to and being controlled by the dead – at a time when women were particularly targeted for having ideas beyond themselves – was easily misunderstood by those outside the spiritualist movement of the nineteenth century. The Christian Church, the new science of Psychology and, in part, the leaders of the British art world looked upon these practices unfavourably and condemned the methods that mediumistic artists used. As this chapter unfolds we shall see how a highly talented spiritualist and artist coped with the rigour of the art world and the problems inherent in dark spirit séances.

Anna Mary Howitt was a trained artist and a psychic medium. According to the historian and writer Joy Dunicliff, she was raised in the Quaker House in Bridge Street, Uttoxeter, Staffordshire, where her parents were Elders. Thus her early spiritual background was that of a Plain Quaker due to the influence of her well-respected literary parents. In an autobiography by her mother, Mary Howitt, it is written that Anna Mary became a spiritualist in her late twenties but had trained as an artist from childhood, like many young middle-class women of the Victorian era, in sketching and watercolour painting. Her parents furthered her education in painting and drawing skills by sending her to be instructed in Heidelberg, Germany, where women were accepted as artists unlike in London at this time. Then from the age of twenty-six she studied in Munich under the tutelage of Wilhelm von Kaulbach (1805-1874), who was known as "a painter famous for his gargantuan canvasses illustrating Biblical and mythical themes."[8] Here she created some of her best works, especially the images in her illustrated book *An Art-Student in Munich* (1853).

---

[8] *A Tale of Two Artists: Anna Mary's Portrait of John Banvard* (J Hanners, Minnesota History, Vol. 50:5, 1987)

Her art training continued at the Henry Sass Art School in Bloomsbury where she was involved with other female artists such as Joanna Mary Boyce and Barbara Bodichon. These women shared similar aims, wishing to progress as artists in the British art scene alongside the male artists of their acquaintance. As well as these highly motivated women, the Howitt family were also acquainted with writers and artists such as William Wordsworth, Charles Dickens, Elizabeth Barrett Browning, Elizabeth Gaskell and members of the Pre-Raphaelite Brotherhood, especially Dante Gabriel Rossetti and John Everett Millais. Anna Mary was also influenced by the Victorian art critic and family friend John Ruskin (1819-1900); as a child, she had demonstrated her drawing skills to him during informal lessons he had given her and he remarked that she had some artistic talent.

Although a talented artist, her chance of success in the Victorian art world was small. Whilst painting and drawing was predominately a pastime for many young middle-class women, the late eighteen-sixties did see female artists gradually being acknowledged by the art world; but even so, women were rarely recognised formally as skilful artists. Art historian Deborah Cherry asserts[9] that it was only by attending the Royal Academy School of Art that women gained credibility in the Victorian art world. Even though Anna Mary's training in Germany helped her to create her large-scale oil painting *Boadicea Brooding over her Wrongs* (1856), entered to the Royal Academy Exhibition in London, as a woman it was impossible to be accepted as an art student there until at least 1860.

Before this date the RA only accepted the best of male British art in their exhibitions, and the dismissal of an artist's painting would naturally influence their reputation and confidence. Moreover, those leading the art world accepted little innovative work, such as the Pre-Raphaelite movement, unless it was 'fine

---

[9] *Painting Women: Victorian Women Artists* (D Cherry, Routledge, 1985)

art', had been through the rigour of being accepted by the RA and was collectable. In fact, a friend of Anna Mary's, Laura Herford (1831-1870), was the first woman to gain a place in 1860 by passing her paintings off as L Herford Esq. i.e. a man!

Simply put, female artists at this time in history were assumed to be less gifted than their male counterparts. Once accepted, even by default, women did begin to gain just a toehold in this masculine dominated Victorian art culture although an exhibition of feminine painting before 1900 was a rare event. This was due in part to the attitude of John Ruskin, who didn't believe that women should write for a living or be trained as serious artists. With his power to build up an artist's reputation, he must have been an intimidating force to women who wished to exhibit their art to the general public.

Anna Mary Howitt, however, was raised to be independent; she expected to work and was heralded as an artist and writer by her well-known parents. This freedom was unusual during a time in social history when middle-class women were not even expected to work. Throughout her lifetime, any artworks created by women received very little public exposure.

Ruskin, on the other hand, was himself interested in Spiritualism and sat in séances with many notable artists including the Pre-Raphaelite, Rossetti. But despite this, and being a friend of the Howitt family, he did not encourage their daughter's spiritual interests and attempted to guide her as an artist by suggesting that she draw and paint still life or subjects from nature. As a trained artist, this could well have seemed insulting and in conflict with her potential talent. For Ruskin, her canvasses did not have the qualities of the "truths of art" that he looked for in a painting. These truths he called "beauty and nature; colour and tone; chiaroscuro and the truth of space (depending on the power of the eye)."[10] Unfortunately, it seems

---

[10] *Modern Painters, Vol. 1:13* (J Ruskin, George Allen, 1847)

that she did not follow his advice since her bold representation of Boadicea from mythical source was rejected by the RA in 1856. Ruskin said that this was because the painting was "Botany, not Art"!

Ruskin may have been influenced by the disappointments of his own séance experiences. He had sat with some of the most noted mediums of the nineteenth century, such as the Scottish levitation medium Daniel Dunglas Home (1833-1896), yet received no definitive evidence of his deceased young love, Rose La Touche. He remarked to his spiritualist friend, Georgina Cowper-Temple, "I was always ready to accept miracles… if only I could get clear and straightforward human evidence of it." Ruskin dearly wanted a message from Rose, a young Irishwoman he had been romantically attached to since her childhood. Affected by her mother's distrust of the ageing Ruskin, and her own confusion, Rose wasted away possibly due to an eating disorder at the age of twenty-seven, with the alleged love affair unresolved. Ruskin was never satisfied by any spiritualist messages through prominent mediums and remained a sceptic.

Of course, the Boadicea painting was her own work, influenced by her tutors, and not controlled by any supernatural influence (which came later) apparently to the detriment of her development as an artist. Anna Mary was a strong-willed woman and a leading feminist, determined to exhibit alongside her male friends despite her gender. But unfortunately, the dismissal of her painting by the select committee of the RA, and Ruskin's criticism, seem to have hurt her sensibilities as an artist and it was said by her mother that she would never paint again. Mary Howitt was very worried about her daughter, as her progress as an artist halted. Almost as a memorial to her, and perhaps to spirit art too, she argued[11] that new genres in the art schools and exhibitions were lacking just because there were no female artists exhibiting.

---

[11] *An Autobiography* (Mary Howitt, Isbister and Company, 1889)

She commented on the absence of insight by the Royal Academy and their lack of up-to-date thinking in neither accepting her daughter nor the Pre-Raphaelite Brotherhood as exhibitors. In 1851, the recently appointed President of the RA, Sir Charles Eastlake, had said that it would be the last year they admitted this "outrageous new school of painting" to their walls. It is shocking to think now that the Brotherhood's paintings changed the face of British art a few years later; one wonders what spirit art could have achieved had it had been accepted too.

Through her parents, Anna Mary became known to the Pre-Raphaelite Brotherhood, in particular Dante Gabriel Rossetti and his wife Elizabeth Siddal. They, along with John Ruskin, would sit in séance to 'commune with the spirits'.[12] A small illustration on black-edged mourning stationery confirms Anna Mary's involvement with the Brotherhood in what appears to be a quick ink sketch by Rossetti. It shows a slight, wasp-waisted woman, her hands raised as though in surprise or about to speak; her left leg is defined by the dark shadowing along the drape of her skirt; her right foot is positioned dramatically as though moving forward to make a point. It is a sure-handed drawing and, although incomplete, Anna Mary's presence is acutely suggested within it. There is a sense of her being a young woman who could attract attention to herself, thus seemingly out of harmony with Victorian female etiquette. The sketch also suggests that Rossetti was a close friend.

By 1859 Anna Mary had married Alaric Alfred Watts (1825-1901), who was a spiritualist and this is when her spiritual work began. With guidance from her new husband, she began sitting regularly in séances and producing automatic writing and small watercolour paintings that she believed were created by the spirit presences controlling her.

---

[12] *The Traveller on the Hill-Top: Mary Howitt* (Joy Dunicliff, Churnet Valley Books, 1998)

It was believed that these presences could use the energies of sitters, who sat without light or heat in order to get a glimpse of the spirits, a touch from them, to receive gifts of objects as apports passed through walls or ceiling or hear rappings on the door or furniture like those experienced in Hydesville. Sitters thought that regular meetings with the spirit world would enable better communications, so Anna Mary, as a developing medium, would sit in these dark séances with her family, her husband and sometimes the friends she had made among spiritualists and artists or writers. The darkness of the séance became her home where she could draw and paint without criticism; it was only in this 'dark world of the light' that she could really demonstrate her gifts of mediumship and art.

Whilst supporting her as an artist, her mother sensed that there was something in this practice that her daughter did not recognise – and which those of influence in the visual arts disliked. Wisely, her mother was concerned that her daughter was delving into the spirit world too often and remarked in her autobiography that "she would have drawn and painted better without the inspiration of the spirits!" This seems to be a concerned comment from a mother who feared her daughter had taken a step too far into the unknown, perhaps knowing that it could destroy her daughter as a recognised artist because of her involvement with Spiritualism.

"Our daughter had, both by her pen and pencil, taken her place amongst the successful artists and writers of the day when, in the spring of 1856, a severe private censure of one of her oil paintings by a king among critics so crushed her sensitive nature as to make her yield to the bias for the supernatural, and withdraw from the ordinary arena of the fine arts. After her marriage to her contemporary and friend from childhood, Alaric Watts, they both jointly pursued psychic studies…

"In the spring of 1856 we had become acquainted with several most ardent and honest spirit mediums. It seemed right, to my husband and myself, to see and try to understand the true nature of these phenomena in which our new acquaintances so firmly believed. In the month of April, I was therefore invited to a séance at Professor de Morgan's and was much astonished and affected by communications purporting to come to me from my dear son Claude… I felt thankful for the assurance thus gained of an invisible world, but resolved to neglect none of my common duties for Spiritualism."

We can see from Mary's writings that the drawings and paintings emerging from her daughter's new world did not suit Ruskin, "a king among critics", as his definition of greatness in art was not that which Anna Mary was creating.

Before Anna Mary's sudden death in 1884, her mother and father sat in several séances with their daughter. They had become involved because of their friendship with the Wilkinsons but towards the end of the century they seemed disillusioned and returned to their work as Quakers. However, even in the early days, Mary felt that involvement with these practices would not be in her daughter's interest, explaining that, "The rapping spirits go on rapping, and people [still] listen to them. I think it is a delusion." With her daughter being married to a spiritualist, this issue may well have caused some friction between the two women.

Her father was also concerned about his daughter's welfare, writing on her forty-fifth birthday in 1869 to warn that, although he accepted a life beyond death, he felt that what a person did while alive on Earth was more important than communicating with the dead. He maintained that, "With all this queerness of Spiritualism and spiritualists, this dispensation to us [as Quakers] [is] the fact of our earth-pilgrimage." In other words, his belief as a Quaker was one of earthly goodness and not of consistent communication with the dead.

Anna Mary, however, ignored her parents' concerns for both her reputation and her art. For her, what happened in

1856 was decisive and she gave up her artistic career. However, we now know that she did continue to paint and draw until her death of tuberculosis in 1884, because the night before she died she sketched the landscapes at Meran in the South Tyrol. But her spirit art was not mentioned again after her parents' comments.

Since she was unable to attend the greatest art school in England because she was a woman, and being rejected by the Royal Academy because critics decided that she was not proficient as an academic artist, possibly she thought that the uniqueness of spirit art was her only way forward as an artist. Yet the uncertainty of 'sitting in dark rooms communicating with invisible beings' was a major reason why spirit art would not be recognised in the nineteenth century by the establishment.

Anna Mary's first spirit drawings indicate that she worked automatically, as did William Martin Wilkinson and John Spear. This is illustrated by the drape of the woman's skirt in her untitled drawing of 'woman and child' (graphite pencil on cartridge paper). Her ability to be able to expose her mind to an extra-sensory form of suggestion – by what she believed to have been a deceased spirit – is demonstrated by scratchy writing overlaying the image. This drawing characterises a woman comforting a child, but legible within it is a form of script that shows her use of automatic writing. When a medium submits their mind 'to the will of a spirit' and writes without thinking, this is usually the forerunner of mediumistic automatism in art. Letting go of one's motor co-ordination is one thing, but an acclaimed artist accepting the controlling will of an unknown force is another. The process of apparent control by the spirit world is difficult to accept, yet it was at this point, as her submission to Spirit became stronger, that her understanding of art changed.

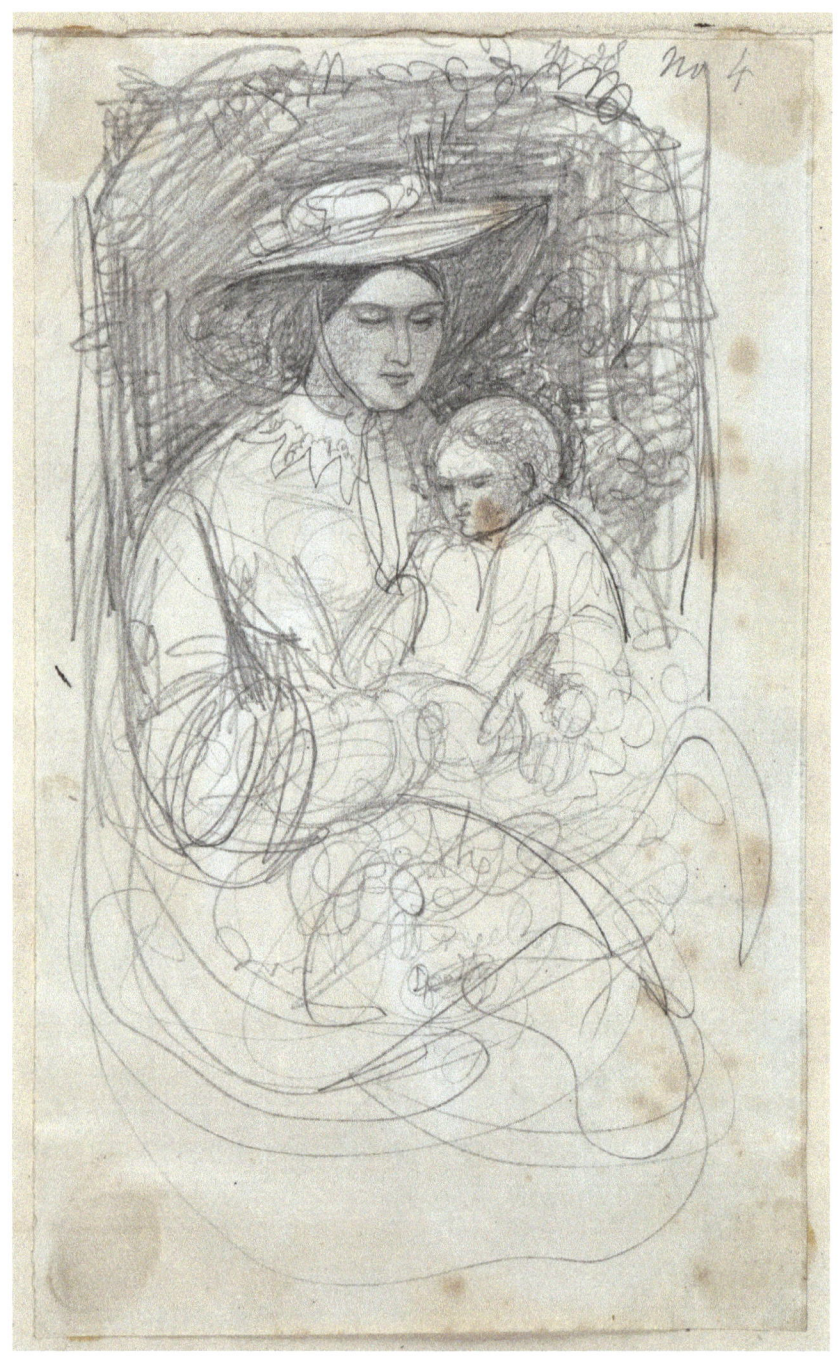

Untitled ('Woman and Child')

This drawing also illustrates Anna Mary Howitt's proficient drawing skill by her use of highlighting the image with a varied backdrop of light to grey to black tones, very different from her non-spiritual work. Whilst the tones have not been darkened by crosshatching, which was popular in Victorian art schools, the darker areas have been constructed by a kind of automatic writing, using words and marks to darken the image. Victorian art students were taught a method of creating an illusion of shadow by overlaying, or crosshatching, graphite pencil marks rather than pressing harder on the paper, as is a modern method. The overlapping of automatic writing produced a series of tones creating light and shade. This technique is a hybrid of automatic writing and automatic drawing, whereby the spirit influence could produce legible texts by prompting the medium's brain to write and then draw. Anna Mary's use of overlaid letterings and words was very unusual, as though she were trying to break through the stiff Victorian art boundaries.

The image suggests that it was created by her hand, using the automated technique, but that these are not her words. Looking closely at the script, it seems to be directed by a 'holy spirit' or 'spirit guide' because the words are written within her drawing. The image has echoes of Christian iconography, that of the Mother and Child. But, puzzlingly, it also appears to be a replica of the artist's own illustration from *An Art Student in Munich* (c.1854), which she created *before* she married and came into Spiritualism. So was this spirit-inspired automated drawing done separately and as an afterthought? Any trained artist will sketch before producing completed paintings, so perhaps here we see personal art and spirit art each inspiring the other.

There is, however, a distinction between the art she made through spirit-control and her personal work, a difference in both content and style. Her own art demonstrates a maturity of technique and style whilst the spirit-controlled drawings and paintings are predominately naïve, reflecting perhaps a cultured tendency towards the content and style of William Blake's illustrations. In her formative years she might have studied Blake and his series of visionary portraits of deceased people which he entitled *Visionary Heads* (c.1818). Like Blake's drawings, Anna Mary's reflected religious themes.

On the 11th May, 1854, the New York Times described her work (*An Art Student in Munich*) as having "a beautiful earnestness and… simplicity that have a talismanic affect upon the reader. It is one of those sunny works which leave a luminous trail behind them in the reader's memory." The use of the word 'talismanic' in this review suggests that her art work already had a mystical quality before her involvement with Spiritualism. In the opinion of the New York Times, her work transcended the normal and she had an innate ability to recreate a person's invisible persona.

By attending séances later, Anna Mary undoubtedly felt a new freedom, one that was not afforded to women in public and social life. It gave her an opportunity to explore abstract and invisible supernatural forces that seemed to stimulate her artistic style in new ways. In believing that these art works were created not by the artist but by guiding spirits, literally any form of art could be produced. (Indeed, the works of Georgiana Houghton, described in Chapter Two, were so non-representational that Victorian art criticism was at a loss to understand them at all.)

A comparison of Anna Mary's mediumistic art with her personal work, such as the oil painting *John Banvard* (1849) and illustrations for *The English Garden at Munich* (1881), shows that she had the confidence and ability to create fine art, which her spirit art works do not appear to have. The first of these was described by art historian John Hanners as "subtle in colour and smooth in execution." His description confirms that she was sophisticated in her use of colour, composition, proportion and painterly process. On the other hand, her spirit drawings produced a decade later appear awkward and tentative, often unfinished and fragile. These small drawings and paintings have little visual strength compared with the large *Banvard* oil painting.

These distinctions are difficult to assess since there is little left of her own artwork to examine, though it is evident that her conventional artworks are very different in style, composition and subject matter. This may have had something to do with her health. John Hanners maintains that Anna Mary had a "mental breakdown" after her rejection by the RA and that she never really recovered from that disappointment. Ruskin, as mentioned before, also doubted her work as an artist in her own right. It would be understandable that she would then give her artistic abilities to the spirits of the séance, since the spirits did not criticise this art.

Victorian séance conditions were cold and dark, in blacked-out rooms often with no fire or gas lamp, and the only sense experiences were rappings or banging, scents, touches or vibrations. But sitters would have heard the scratching of Anna Mary's pencil as she facilitated the spirit drawing of images. It seems incredible that a woman would give her physical body over to unseen spirits in this way, at a time when women were socially, physically and emotionally repressed by men.

The spirit influence in Anna Mary Howitt's drawings is illustrated in her portrait of a boy surrounded by swirls of leaves and flowers. The postcard-sized drawing appears unfinished as though the 'guidance' left her before its completion. When I examined it, at Cambridge University, I felt it possible that the face is that of her beloved brother Claude, who had died aged ten in 1844. The tiny image seems to pull the viewer into the minute detail of the face, perhaps not for aesthetic reasons but to enable a better view of the child. The pencil work is lightly overlaid with marks showing outlines of foliage popular in female Victorian drawing. The cherub-like portrait was created by 'smudging', a technique of tempering the edges of the slightly textured cartridge paper to enable a younger, softer appearance; the face tonally formed gives the illusion that the boy is emerging out of the cartridge paper, perhaps away from physical death into spirit life.

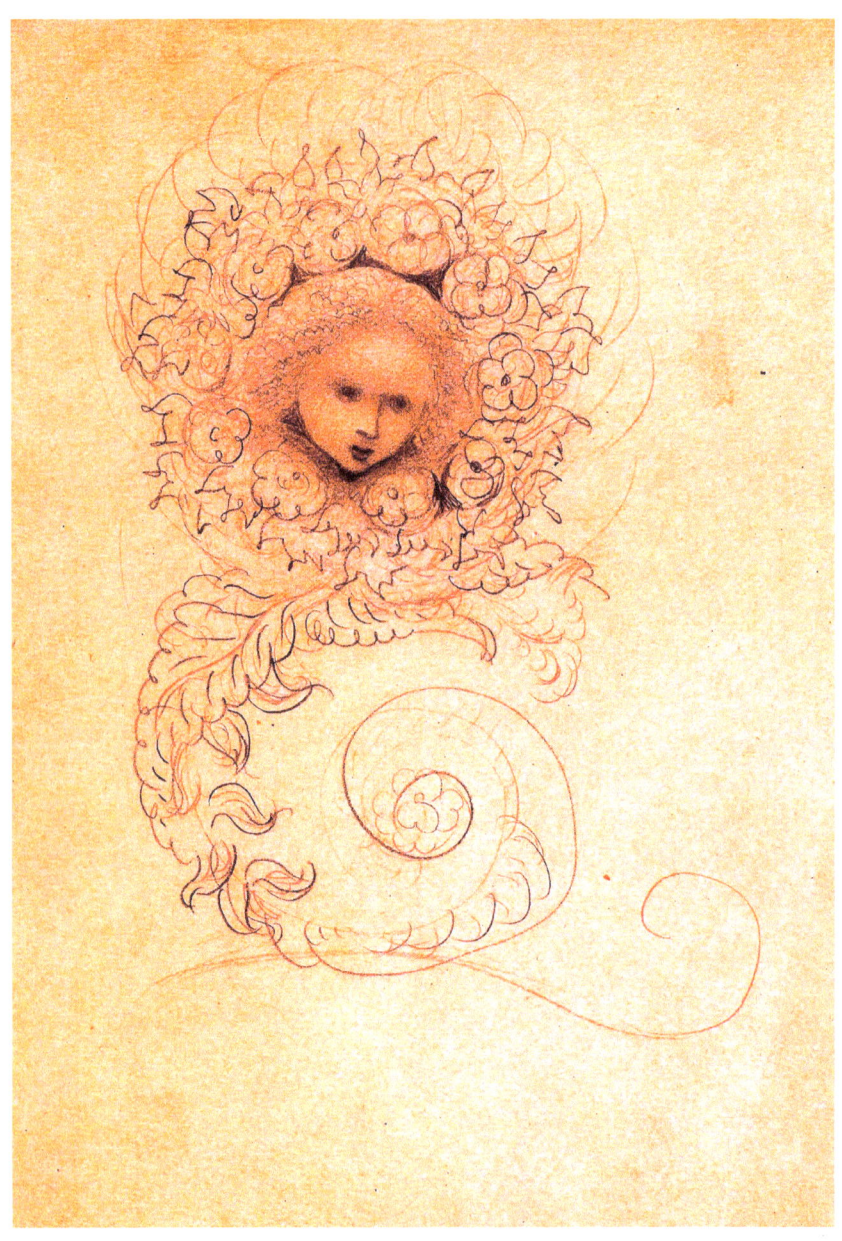

Untitled ('Boy')

Mary Howitt, the boy's mother, had received many messages from Claude when she attended séances with the mathematician Augustus de Morgan, so it is possible that Anna Mary created this small portrait from a memory of her brother, and arguably not by spirit influence. She certainly believed that her art was created in amanuensis by 'a holy being', in much the same way as mid-nineteenth century Shakers believed that their artistic inspiration came directly from the 'invisible presence of God'. Since Shaker art had been produced from the early eighteen-thirties, there is also a possibility that her spirit drawings were influenced by this, following her visit to America in 1848-9. This sacred belief in God and holy beings is noticeable in all her spirit art, whether entirely influenced by the spirits of the deceased or not. But she was known to have over-drawn or over-painted her work after a séance had closed, thus transferring the 'ownership' from the spirits to herself.

As far as we know, Anna Mary had few allies to support her spirit work. Ruskin's scepticism of it led her to conceal her work, which was then donated to Cambridge University Library and left unseen for many years in back rooms. This archive consists of delicate drawings and watercolour paintings, thirty-one of her spiritual artworks from about 1859-1880; they have lain almost unnoticed, and now discoloured by time, coiled up in faded Victorian packages and tied with fraying string, attracting little attention from the public or academia.

Most of these watercolour paintings and drawings are small in size, no bigger than A4 and no smaller than a postcard. The sketching is incomplete, whilst the paintings defined by opaque contrasts of colour and tone seem unfinished as though quickly drafted suggesting that, once the drawings were produced, the creative energy dissipated from the work. Anna Mary's spirit paintings and drawings were inextricably linked to her belief that life exists after death, but they are also marked by a lack of craftsmanship in comparison with her previous conventional art work which had advocated an unorthodox approach towards painting. Bessie

Parkes Belloc commented that her work was "…some of the most delicate, beautiful drawings ever done by a woman's hand."

But several people noted that, on becoming a spiritualist, her personality, behaviour and mental capabilities changed as she grew older working with the spirits. By the end of 1870, the perceptive critic William Michael Rossetti would write in his diary that she "does not now pursue art under the form of 'spirit drawings'." He went on to say later that, "…if only the spirits had let her alone, she would have drawn and painted much better than she ever did under their inspiration." Eventually her spirit muses deserted her and she stopped altogether. By 1879, now fifty-five years old, Anna Mary Howitt was described by John Hanners as "cracked."

Sadly, the spirits she believed in presented a real conundrum for Victorian psychology. Rachel Oberter has suggested that the mind of a mentally ill person can believe that they have famous or divine personalities speaking to them; thus at least some nineteenth-century spirit art might have been created through the artists' imagination and not by the hand of spirit. The question of imagination versus belief has to remain unanswered[13], but it is certain that Anna Mary's reaction to the art establishment's dismissal of her personal work affected her deeply.

We have an insight to her beliefs, for example about Christianity and the presence of angels, in one of her images that shows a tableau of a small white-winged figure floating on a white cloud. It is painted in Indian-red watercolour to the bottom right of the left part of the diptych. Like William Blake's etchings, this is a small image (about seven by nine inches) in which the top right-hand figure is lit from all angles and seemingly transparent; it gives the effect of calling, with a gesture, to those below, inferring a hierarchical order to the painting.

---

[13] As will be shown later, modern spirit art may at least have 'evidence' in the form of photographs in order to support its beliefs and philosophy. A form of photography only began to become widely available in the 1840s but, in any case, the spirit art being produced in the nineteenth century was not intended to be evidential in this sense.

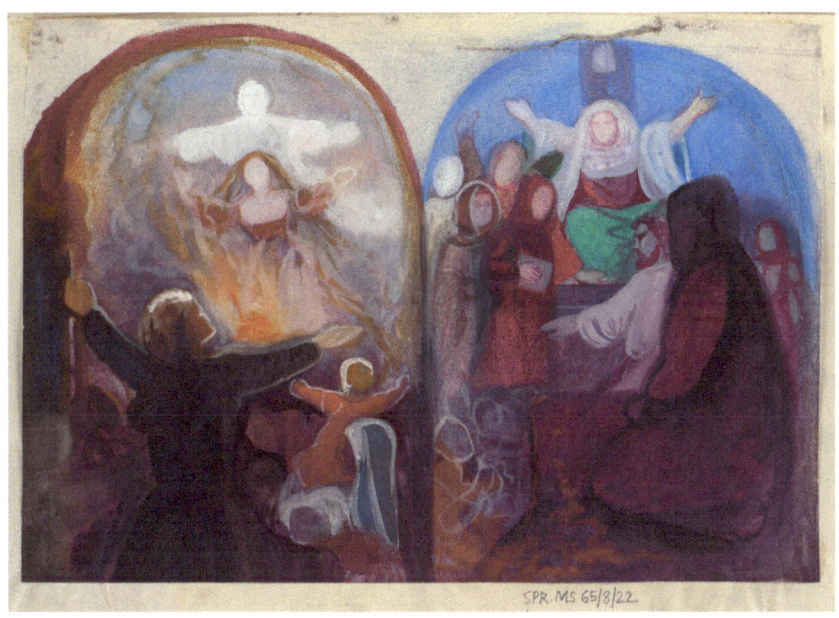

Untitled watercolour diptych

The darkened colours and tones of purple and blue may represent humanity reaching out from the darkness of physical existence to a heavenly spiritual light. The gold and silver hues seem to characterise 'higher forces' whilst the white, ghostlike figures with their faceless shapes illustrate her interpretation of the passage from life to death, from the dark to the light of Spirit. All these elements signify both spiritualist and Christian views of the existence of Heaven, reminiscent of Blake's *Book of Job* or the illustrations for his *Mind-Forg'd Manacles*, replicating the subjugation of the human spirit within the body.

Some of Anna Mary's paintings contain Christian symbolism, rather like a tableau from a theatre set. Dark-hooded figures (perhaps representative of 'low', unspiritual people?) evoke echoes of Renaissance paintings used as visual allegories; art works would often tell stories for the illiterate. In the painting mentioned, the upper segment on the left side of the diptych appears to signify the Christian idea of Heaven (Spirit), whereas the lower shows Hell (the Earth). Here, the linear use of opaque Chinese-white paint boosts the scene's storyline as visual agents; the holy imagery of open-armed subjects, assuming the pose of feminine Christ-like figures, beckon the lower people forward into the light.

Laura Schneider Adams[14] employs Jacques Derrida's 'order of fiction' in arguing that images in artwork above the middle of the painting represent the 'spiritual / saved / good / weightless / light' whilst the lower images represent the 'damned / evil / weighed down / darkness'. She proposes that the fresco *The Last Judgement* by Giotto (1267-1337) is an example of this form of spiritual perspective. Anna Mary's painting shows the same understanding of a spiritual order by using colour as well as light: the lighter tones are 'up' whilst the darker colours are 'down'. (In contemporary spiritual artwork, this colour system often remains similar.) It is known that Anna Mary received instruction on colour from Gabriel Rossetti, who wrote to his sister Christina in 1853 that he was visiting her studio for this reason.

This diptych demonstrates that she fully understood how colour could affect an audience: the lighter hues higher as a representation of spirituality, the darker ones lower to illustrate those lacking spirituality. Howitt appears to be identifying spiritual energies in her séance pictures; this painting is understood by spiritualists to have been created automatically using spirit possession.

Could it be that this painting also informs us about her feminist thoughts? The dominant white figure appears to represent a female 'higher being' who motions to the 'lower' humans, this at a time in history when women were in the main subjugated by men. Such a representation is most unusual. The people depicted here reflect her sensitivity to the existence of an earthly darkness that surrounded women, and an opposition to Victorian social attitudes, by illustrating two women at higher spiritual levels to their male counterparts.

---

[14] *The Methodologies of Art: An Introduction* (L Schneider Adams, Westview Press, 2010)

It is possible that Anna Mary's own religious and feminist beliefs and values may have contributed to these images and unconsciously influenced her artwork. Whilst using Christian storylines, such as the open-armed Christ-like figure, she has identified the body as female to infer that women are equal to men in terms of spiritual values. For a woman to paint a female Christ at this time would have been a brave step and maybe one too far for the Church of England, challenging the accepted gender conventions of the time. This could also be read as a cry for equality for women. Victorian thought did not accept this idea, so it could be that her art was deliberately held back by a male-dominated establishment.

Art historian Rachel Oberter has suggested that the idea of a feminine deity is "neither simply metaphysical nor unique" since Florence Nightingale, who lived at the same time as Howitt, also referred to Christ as an asexual being. This anomalous spiritual entity preoccupied Anna Mary the medium. Given that she was brought up in a Quaker family and would have received her spirituality from that source, her interest in Christ-like figures would be normal and fit with Christian Spiritualism.

Yet at this time women were not only subordinate to men but subject to the teachings of the Church of England.[15] By creating spirit art, which also included feminist overtones, Anna Mary Howitt may well have damaged her own reputation and allowed doubts to arise over her sanity. It is certainly true that the Church of England became concerned for the minds of its ladyfolk as they began to attend the darkened rooms of the séances.[16]

Upon setting foot there, female artists were entering an imaginary and sacred space, where the invisible hands of believed controlling etheric beings guided them in their 'Heaven' to create

---

[15] *Victorian Feminism 1850-1900* (Philippa Levine, Hutchinson Education, 1987)
[16] *The Other World: Spiritualism and Psychical Research in England 1850-1914* (Janet Oppenheim, Cambridge University Press, 1985)

writings and drawings. For these women, the séance room was a neutral space that provided freedom and safety from any male oppression experienced in their life outside.

Anna Mary died at the age of fifty-nine, four years before her mother. She was an artist who came into Spiritualism, leaving her personal art behind, just as women were beginning to be accepted into higher education and the exhibiting art world. She was a talented artist in her own right, but after being dismissed by the Royal Academy she turned to the art of spirit.

Here she found an outlet for her strong belief in God, in the angels and in a spirit world, transforming her gifts as an artist and leading her closer to the meaning of her God.

Georgiana Houghton, on the other hand, created drawings and paintings using mediumistic automatism in a totally different manner, and attempted to bring her works to public view where she could sell them.

2

Nineteenth Century Automatism and Abstraction

Spirit art did not flourish in the galleries and art establishments of Victorian Britain, perhaps due to the manner in which it was created. Yet these pioneer artists risked social status and possible accusations of insanity in their determination to provide evidence of a spirit world. We are describing here two very different women whose artwork was equally diverse: but whilst Anna Mary Howitt's figurative art was generally hidden away from the public eye, Georgiana Houghton wished her highly abstracted work to be shown. Indeed, she organised a large exhibition at the New British Gallery in Bond Street, London, in 1871.

In recent years, more has been learned about the life and work of Georgiana which makes study and research easier. Her major works are housed in the Victorian Spiritualist Union, Melbourne, but have been loaned out for exhibition at the Courtauld Institute of Art, London. They are extraordinary impressions of the spirit world, appearing almost totally abstract. Strata of watercolour paint have been built up as each layer dried, creating symbols suggestive of the energy that the human form exudes at death and beyond. This art was before its time, before abstraction was first created by mainstream artists and before impressions of spirit life were considered worthwhile in Spiritualism. Her paintings simply illustrated energy. She had no preconception as to what the paintings would look like since many were created in total darkness, under the control of her artist 'guides', and the sensations she received were magnified as symbolic colour.

Georgiana was born in 1814 in Las Palmas de Gran Canaria and moved to London with her family in 1830. This relocation was possibly due to political unrest in Spain that made it difficult for her father to work and maintain eleven children (two of whom died in childhood). Her siblings included a sister Zilla (1820-1851) whom Georgiana thought a better artist than herself. In fact, Georgiana gave up her art training after Zilla's death, transferring her art skills to Spiritualism. Art and death, for some, were becoming interesting bedfellows. Other early deaths in the family included a brother Cecil Angelo, sisters Helen and Julia, then Warrand, Sidney Alexander and George Clarence.

Their mother was Ann Mary Houghton, née Warrand (1784-1869), and their father was George Houghton (1778-1863), a trading merchant. He transported sherry and wines from Spain and the Canary Islands to Britain and Europe. In 1863, the family moved from 5 Upper Craven Place, Highgate Road in Kentish Town, London, after an accident that exacerbated George Houghton's death. The family were in some financial difficulty and moved to Delamere Crescent, Westbourne Square, London, where Georgiana lived as a spinster with her elder brother Charles and other members of the family. Ann Mary died six years after her husband.

While the family was together, Georgiana's parents supported her financially but after their deaths her life became both socially and financially difficult. As a single woman she sought financial help from her eldest brother, who declined. This was very unfortunate since Victorian class structure was determined by the work and status of the parents, or of the men in the family, and it was common for unmarried middle-class women to rely on support from the father or brother in the family.

Thus she had to rely on earnings by any work she managed to acquire and would have known that the middle classes had the money to pay for spirit messages through mediumship. It is also possible that the many deaths of her siblings might have been a stimulus for Houghton to work as a medium and spirit artist (she had attended her first séance in 1851). These circumstances differentiated her social status and standing from that of Anna Mary Howitt. The historian Alex Owen describes her as a "domestic medium", implying that her social standing was between the worlds of the working and the middle classes.[17]

Although Georgiana Houghton had received a year of formal art training before her father died, she did not have the extensive instruction in the European or English art colleges as had Howitt. An artist who has been trained can recognise whether a drawing is technically right or not and so is able to correct their work. Anna Mary Howitt was able to do this, including for her spirit watercolours, but Georgiana Houghton did not have the same artistic understanding or technical resource. Thus her abstracted work, although very interesting and the first of its kind, was not as aesthetically competent as Anna Mary's.

John Ruskin noted that an artist's ability to assess visually and make changes to their work was a skill that competent artists innately understood. In *Modern Painters* he called this process "judgement" – the ability to judge whether a drawing or painting was created using "a high form of intelligence". This notion of judgement negated Georgiana's art since the standard of her

---

[17] *The Darkened Room: Women, Power and Spiritualism in Late Victorian England* (Alex Owen, Virago Press, 1989)

work could not be judged in the same way as others'.[18] Georgiana commented on this in her 1881 autobiography (see footnote 6) when she wrote:

"For the [spirit] drawing phase, I was prepared by my own earthly training, having devoted the chief part of my life to that accomplishment, until Zilla's death in 1851 so crushed me that I felt as if I should never again use a pencil or brush."[19]

She was sadly and deeply affected by Zilla's sudden death and from that date began to believe in the "possibility of communication with the spirits of those who had passed away from the mortal form." She began sitting for half an hour each evening to obtain the gift of mediumship but it was not until 1859 that she began to produce drawings by spirit guidance; already a medium, she just needed an artist guide to help her make the spirit-inspired drawings through her, using the slight art skills she had.

At first she attempted to gain mediumistic inspiration from Zilla, but found from her 'contact' with Zilla that it was their deceased brother Cecil who guided her. It was he who informed her spiritually, she believed, but she also realised that she could connect with a deceased deaf and dumb artist known as Henry Lenny. Lenny assisted with her first drawings, then five years later she reported that she was guided by 'higher beings' such as the Christian saint, John. It is unclear whether these changes of spirit guidance were deliberate, though it is likely that she would have earned more from her sittings with moneyed middle class patrons if her guides had Christian status. She explained her development in her *New British Gallery Exhibition Catalogue* (1871), produced for her first exhibition:

"In July, 1861, I heard of Mrs Wilkinson's spirit drawings, so on the evening of the 20th I asked [the spirits] whether my sister Zilla, who had been an accomplished artist while upon the Earth, could guide my hand for spiritual work, but neither she nor my

---

[18] *Modern Painters: John Ruskin* (David Barrie, ed., Andre Deutsch Ltd, 1989)
[19] Reprinted by Fb&c Ltd, 2017

brother Cecil (whom I had asked [for] as he was about the same age as Mrs Wilkinson's young son, who was her guiding spirit) could be permitted to do it, but Cecil then brought Henry Lenny, who had been a deaf and dumb artist, and he immediately controlled my hand, which was resting on the planchette, to form various curved lines, after which I was impressed to remove the black lead pencil and replace it with a blue one, with which he worked upon the same piece of paper, No.1; and I obtained leave to sit every evening for the purpose of drawing."

During her séances she created paintings with little form for the eye to grasp: they were predominately abstract with swirling images, far from straightforward, yet Georgiana could read a story in the non-representational strokes of the pencil or brush. In this way, Georgiana continued her mediumship through art. The spirit messages she delivered to her patrons provided her with an income of approximately one or two guineas for a reading or drawing. Once established as a reliable spiritualist medium, the rich and upper classes began visiting her at her London home and with their financial help she gained "status, attention and variety." These benefits became cultural collateral for her, according to Alex Owen, building up her social status and reputation, "important and not unwelcome by-products of psychical gifts."

Georgiana claimed to have enjoyed the attention from wealthy London clients, which she describes in her autobiography. The book is in the form of a diary or journal, where she explicitly names the sitters who attended her séances as well as describing her practices and creative style, a steady flow of impressionist drawings and paintings with mainly mimetic religious themes. Page by page, she reveals the methods of mediumship and drawing processes used during the making of her spirit-controlled art. Her methods were very different in technique, style and use of materials to Anna Mary Howitt's (which may have been, as mentioned, because she was not as competent an artist). The differences make the styles of the two artists' paintings and drawings very individual and extraordinary.

Her first drawings were portraits of a visionary nature, as she received ephemeral and non-photographic 'extras'. "One day, accidentally on a blank sheet of paper, she saw upon it a lovely little face… which gradually disappeared…"[20] As these faces occurred she would draw around them, thus producing the first 'evidential' spirit art since the portrait could be recognised by the recipient of the drawing. However, Houghton did not use photographs to demonstrate the evidential nature of her art since, having no particular skill of her own, she just wanted to let the spirits take control. With pencil, crayon or brush in hand, she allowed the planchette to spin around the paper under her guide's influence to create her new style of work. The later drawings for which she is best known became more and more abstract in order to 'tell a story' – rather than offer evidence – with the colours and images produced.

Her individual style of mediumistic automatism shows us that she had strong spiritualist beliefs, willing to let her own will subside and her spirit guides possess her. Her lack of formal art training, moreover, gave her the freedom to create images naturally from her own being, rather than as a result of developed talent or out of fear of the critic. Her spirit art evolved through a series of methods. Initially these were supernatural, without submitting the physical body to control or possession, seeing ghostly impressions of faces on white paper that she then copied by drawing around the image. I would term this 'clairvoyant imagery' whereby, as a medium, she was able to reconstruct only that which she could see on the paper.

Other Victorian drawing mediums who experimented with the processes of spirit art held the belief that their work was actually controlled by spirit forces. Gradually, Georgiana, like the Wilkinson and Howitt families, also developed this skill of mediumistic automatism by submitting to spirit possession. Now known for her highly abstract artworks, unique and original in

---

[20] *Photography and Spirit* (John Harvey, Reaktion Books, 2007)

the mid- to late-Victorian era (just as they are today), she is by no means representative of the conventional Victorian art created during her lifetime. Art historian Rachel Oberter considers her work as "organic" in quality with a sense of "microscopic detail… of being in a deep-sea world or otherwise mysterious place."

A spirit artist myself, I do not regard Georgiana's work like this. I see spacial depths as though her paintings symbolise a realm between Earth and a spirit world, a life-after-death existence. The layers between the many spaces are not solid but appear fluid, as are spirit energies, with each colour representing a spiritual meaning. Mediumistic automatism, the artist suggests, cannot be controlled by the facilitator's mind or the possessed hand but is created by the spirit world; so this art can only be interpreted in spiritual terms and not likened to solid forms as on earthly land or at sea.

Her painting, *The Eye of God*, was the centrepiece of her London exhibition in 1871 and it validates Houghton's belief in the existence of a higher spiritual power as a pure, loving energy. This spiritual power is represented by the peacock feather-like images flowing over the surface of the paper, which are then overlaid by white crystalline forms. This suggests a contest between materialism and spirituality. By making reference to the Book of Job, 31:4, "Doth not he see my ways and count all my steps?" she confirms her belief in higher forces helping her to paint. She explained in her autobiography this need for divine guidance during the preparation of her exhibition. The size, shape, colour and script were all calculated, she says, by her spirit communicators, and she obeyed completely.

"I now had to commence my Catalogue, and to shape the method in which it was to be made out, which required deep consideration and earnest prayer for instruction as to what would be most seemingly, for in that especially I needed divine guidance, and, I am thankful to say, received it fully in every detail." In the 1871 Catalogue itself, she described her art-making process:

"To make the character and design of this Exhibition understood, I must explain that in execution of the Drawings my hand has been entirely guided by Spirits, no idea being formed in my own mind as to what was going to be produced, nor did I know, when a stroke was commenced, whether it would be carried upwards or downwards."

By submitting to these unseen intelligences she believed that her paintings also acquired mystical healing qualities and she reflected that the colours refer to 'states of the soul'. "The unhappy spirits in places of darkness and misery… Spirits of a higher grade… gradually becoming lighter." This colour guidance would later be reflected in the 'auragraphs' created by the Theosophist, Charles Webster Leadbeater (b.1854), in the work of Wassily Kandinsky (b.1866 and said by some to have been the first abstract painter) and in the interpretations of music into colour by Paul Klee (b.1879). Although these artists used some of her methods, none made reference to the religion of Spiritualism or its practices.

Even though her mind communicated with what she believed to be dead spirits, her reputation and mental capacity did not appear to be tarnished, unlike Anna Mary Howitt. Moreover, Houghton was determined to exhibit all her art so that the work would "display the wondrous powers of the unseen intelligences… to manifest unflinchingly to the world of Spiritualism… the religion of the Sacred Scriptures." As one of a few spirit artists in the mid-nineteenth century, she was the only one to exhibit publicly and she herself organised two exhibitions of her spirit-inspired paintings and drawings, in London and in Brighton. There she hung images created during séances between 1861 and 1871, and in her autobiography she declares that her art was acclaimed by the *News of the World* and by *Queen* magazine. But although she had created over five hundred pieces of spirit art in those ten years, and exhibited one hundred and fifty-five paintings and drawings, only one of them was sold. This suggests a lack of general public approval of or interest in spirit art. Only now in the twenty-first century is her art being exhibited in galleries and institutions in major cities.

In the painting *The Flower of Catherine Emily Stringer* (1866), we see the curved strokes of Georgiana's 'guiding spirit', created during one of her séances. Painted on cream paper, there is an undercurrent of out-of-focus green lines demonstrating how the planchette travelled across the surface. Georgiana explained that she felt the pen, brush or pencil change from time to time as her hand, controlled by her guide in the dark, substituted coloured strokes. Overlaid with red and orange and – new to Victorian painting – Chinese opaque white, the painting was created in a matter of minutes, illustrating the energies being released.

The 1871 artworks were, and still are, unique. The impressions of *Spirit Fruits*, *Spirit Flowers* and *The Holy Trinity* appear predominately as soft, spiralling undercurrents of neutral colours overlaid with white, evocative of energies stirring in space. Each colour has a meaning, "given to me by the Spirits, so that, when they use them, they may thus have some insight into the meaning of what is worked through them" and these are referred to on the back of her paintings.

Energies are depicted by colours and shapes, as illustrated for example in *The Eye of God* (c.1856). The undercurrent colours of burnt reds or burnt carmine are symbolic of 'steadfastness' whilst the golden yellows represent 'faith, energy or thoughtfulness'. Georgiana reads these colours as messages from the spirits and through her enigmatic visual creations she assumes the role of educator for those who view her paintings. For example:

The Interpretation of Colours

as represented in spirit flowers, spiritual crowns, monograms, etcetera.

THE ART OF SPIRIT

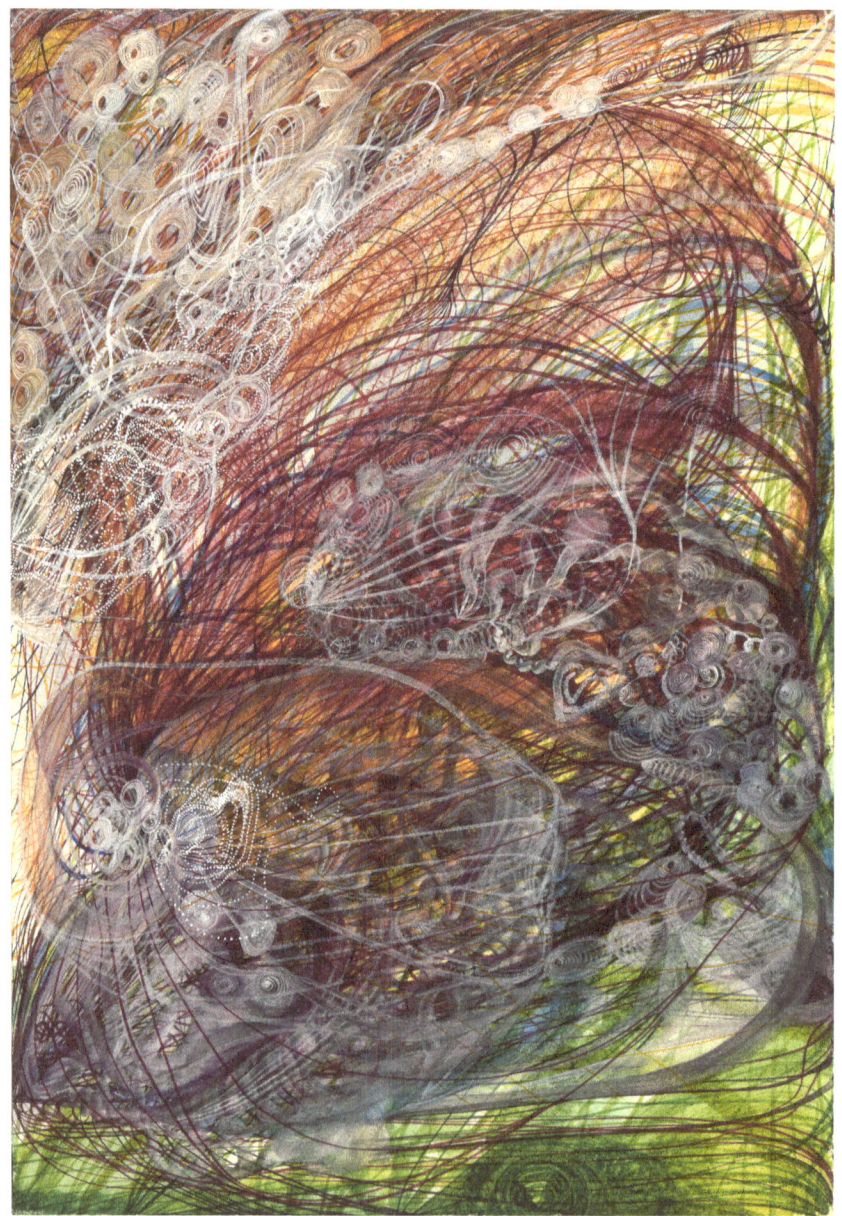

The Flower of Catherine Emily Stringer

- Gamboge… Faith
- Indian Yellow… Probability
- Yellow Ochre… Delicacy of Mind
- Light Amber… Earnestness, etc.

This small sample from her catalogue was among pages and pages of interpretations for the colours that the spirits asked her to paint and describe and they play a considerable part in the meaning of each painting. This was a massive undertaking for her. However, she believed that the spirits owned the art, that they were the agency by which these works were created; they were not formed in her mind first before she began a drawing. We shall see later that modern artists often use the same methodology of interpreting colours in their work, yet without actually knowing where the technique came from.

Houghton also believed that she was an instrument by which deceased artists created new work. She wrote that she wanted her art to be known under the banner of Spiritualism and that her work was not from her mind – as outsider art later became – but from the experience of another soul, a deceased soul. In her book she refers to a query from a visitor regarding how the work was made:

"Mr S, one of my visitors [to the London Exhibition], told me on his first entrance that he must frankly inform me that he was yet on the debatable ground, not having made up his mind as to whether spiritual communication were a fact, or simply self-delusion… On reaching the one numbered 29, he exclaimed, '*That is a proof!* Anyone understanding anything whatever of the subject knows that no artist ever springs *at once* from one method of working to another completely opposite. *That* drawing is by a different hand!' [During] the execution of the drawings, my hand has been entirely guided by spirits, no idea being formed in my own mind as to what was going to be produced."

It seems that Mr S saw differences in the drawing styles displayed in Georgiana's work, as though different artists had created the images and they were not her 'delusion'. According to spirit artists today, the sensation of the body under light or deep control of the spirit who creates the images is referred to as being 'overshadowed'. For example, contemporary spirit artist Paul C describes the feeling as though "my hand does not belong to me as the pencil… sweeps across the paper." Georgiana described a meeting with an artist, Mr L:

"When I had an opportunity of shewing him three distinct stages of work, each of which seemed to fill him with more and more astonishment, I had two drawings in progress, and began upon the one that was nearly finished, so he watched with deep interest the fine lines that went on so smoothly and so unerringly under my hand, never failing to reach exactly their purposed destination, notwithstanding that I was in full conversation with him all the time; and there would be sudden changes of detail, and methods of manipulation, which clearly did not require my mind to be concentrated upon them, which must have been the case had *self* been the operator, even supposing the possibility of my powers being equal to such perfect work."

In other words, because her mind was in conversation with Mr L and her 'self' was preoccupied speaking to him, the spirits must have been guiding her hand. She also addressed the question of possible self-deception when she reported that Mr S at first did not believe that the spirits created the art: "…he wondered if it was self-deception until he saw the work and thus changed his mind."

The two exhibitions were her claim to fame. Nonetheless, selling art with mystical properties proved difficult. From the large London exhibition just one, *The Ear of the Lord* (c.1870)[21], was sold to a Mr Hardwick. These images were exhibited in rented frames and were important to the inquisitive, and yet they lacked

---

[21] The title refers to Psalm 145:18, "The Lord is nigh unto all them that call upon Him, to all that call upon Him in truth." The artist was suggesting that her work was 'the truth' and from the spirits.

critical recognition. The public attitude was perhaps expressed in the report by the *News of the World* (May, 1871):

"An exhibition of a novel character is open in the New British Gallery, 39 Old Bond Street, consisting of drawings by a lady, who states that her hand has been entirely guided by the spirits, no idea being formed in her own mind as to what was being produced... We do not recognise in her extraordinary achievements more than what an accomplished and patient artist... could produce; but her conviction claims respect, and although we have met with nothing to induce us to believe in the spirit theory, we readily acknowledge the thorough conscientiousness of Miss Houghton's belief."

To people who were not spiritualists, Houghton's was a confusing technique. Frederic Myers (1843-1901) attempted to make sense of spirit possession during automatism and trance drawing, writing or speaking, by researching five hundred mediums. He concluded that:

"The difference broadly is, that in Possession the automative's own personality does, for the time, altogether disappear, while there is more or less complete *substitution* of personality, writing or speech being given by spirit through the entrance organism [the medium]." [22]

Myers suggested that a certain part of the medium's personality is retained during the automatism process and not all of the personality is lost or given over to the control of a spirit. Even though Georgiana said she had the ability to stop the spirits from creating art through her, she would not have been aware of Myers' conclusion that the brain can still override that control with 'muscle memory' since she died some twenty years before his study was first made public.

Alex Owen has remarked that Victorian spiritualist mediums often commented that they stood in grave danger of losing their

---

[22] *Human Personality and Its Survival of Bodily Death* (F W H Myers, Longmans Green & Co, 1907; new edition Cambridge University Press, 2011)

personal liberty – their mind and their body – to the spirits. That is, there might have been a risk to the medium's sanity when control by the spirit was so intense that the lucidity of the medium was not as clear as it seemed. Georgiana Houghton, however, believed herself to be protected against undesired spirit possession because she knew how to halt any total control by the spirit. She also believed that she could stop her hand from creating the hysterical "wildly shaking... or manic script" that sometimes occurred during others' spirit-writing (automatism) by terminating any rapidly created drawings. It seems she was determined not to let the spirits get in the way of her earning capacity, such as by being branded as mentally unstable when hand movements were too exaggerated!

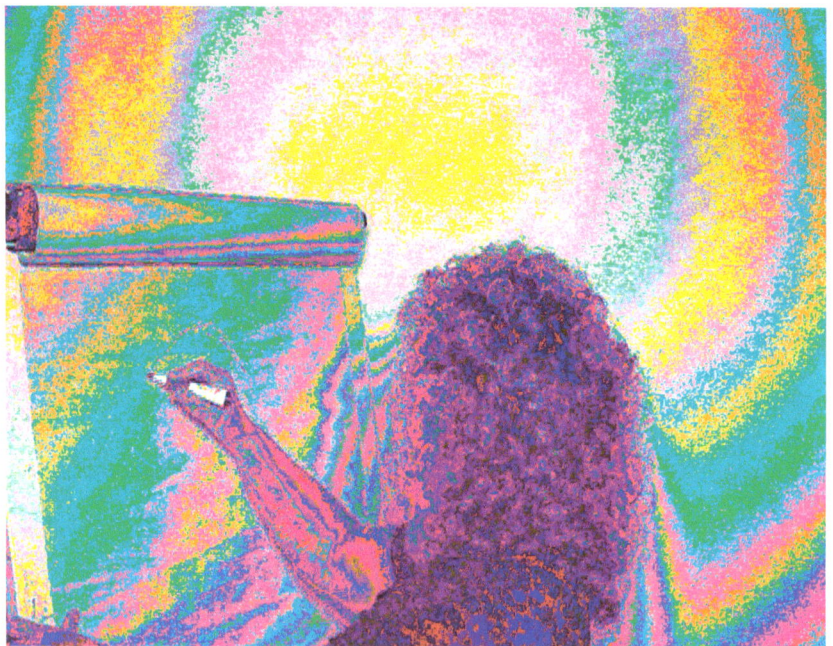

Poly-Interference photograph of aura

The Poly-Interference photograph demonstrates how the psychic energy surrounding a person changes as a spirit artist works. Harry Oldfield, the inventor of this Poly-Interference Photography, realised that people have different energies emanating from them and these could be seen by using technology. (Georgiana's images seem to portray similar coloured energy fields so we may surmise that her art represents the colours of energy and spiritual light that the spirit world 'saw' and painted through her.) From the late 1980s, Oldfield created a scanner that illustrated moment by moment a moving image of one's energy field. Oldfield believed that by studying a person's energy in this way one might better understand health imbalances than by examining the physical body.

The medium and healer, Mark Foster, used this method to photograph the changing energy colours around me as I created a spirit drawing. In a moving film – this image being only one frame of the film – the colours changed remarkably as I worked with the guidance of the spirit world, brightening and becoming almost fluorescent. Then, as the spirit force moved away from me, the colours dimmed. Georgiana Houghton described similar movements of colour while under the inspiration of her spirit guide.

She continued to create abstract paintings to the end of her life. In 1865 one of her pieces was selected by the Royal Academy, but not shown for exhibition, and she continued to submit spirit art to major art critics at a time when the Pre-Raphaelite Brotherhood's work was just becoming accepted. Whilst art establishments were unmoved, she did cite known artists who were interested in her work, in an abbreviated form to hide their identity. These were artists such as 'Mr L' and 'Mr S' who were fascinated by the unorthodox twists and turns of work, when the art world was controlled by the Royal Academy and conventional art criticism.

Her belief that her paintings had the power to heal, and that they had to be viewed and felt by the general public for this to be recognised, was if nothing else an effective marketing ploy to attract people and the Press to her exhibition. Yet she does seem to have been convinced that the energies of the spirits empowered the paint box and the paint, and that these energies could mystically enable communication with the spirits of the deceased.

She even lent her watercolour box to her friends, complete with a 'mystical rag', so that they could experience the healing qualities especially as they used certain colours. She would explain, for example, that the use of orange symbolised 'power' but Chinese orange indicated 'unselfishness'…

"In the hope that many will follow my example, and strive to develop themselves as drawing mediums, I subjoin my list of the interpretation of colours, as given to me by the spirits, so that when they use them they may thus have some insight into the meaning of what is worked through them."

In dark séance rooms, she laid out her watercolour paints, brushes and paper ready for symbiotic meetings with the spirits to occur. Working blind, her hand would move rapidly across the page laying down the first less intense colours under deeper richer tones, completing with opaque whites circling and spiralling on the surface. While she was painting, she would have been aware that she was creating an aura of spirituality around her art; believing that higher level beings came to her through this work, the art was sacred and could affect others in positive and spiritual ways.

Critics like John Ruskin controlled public interest in and the sale of art; for them, spirit art was not a recognised genre and had little value outside Spiritualism. Georgiana Houghton, however, persisted in promoting her work, believing that it was for the good of mankind, despite Ruskin and disenchanted Press reviews. Although the opening of the London exhibition was overflowing, it was mainly the Press who attended with one report suggesting that "troops of fairies have been meandering [over the canvas]." Still, in spite of such condescending remarks, Georgiana was not considered "cracked" as Anna Mary Howitt had been.

She required money to survive but her commercial inexperience was revealed in the exhibition balance sheets: she spent more than she earned from exhibiting. Although she was left in debt, her determination is revealed in her remark that she would have liked a yearly exhibition.

"In my case it certainly has not been a financial success; indeed, I have been a considerable loser… We might hope that each year will diminish the prejudice against Spiritualism, and now that I have ventured to break the ice, it would be a pity to allow the water to freeze over it again."

With little experience of the art world, she appears not to have realised that the reason for an exhibition is to show work to potential buyers; sales would not necessarily be immediate but the event may well lead to other commissions. Some buyers wait for the acute eye of the critic – Ruskin in this case – to qualify the work as a potential asset before purchasing. Although overwhelmed with visitors at the opening evenings, few people visited the exhibitions after that. There was, however, at least one who wished her well…

"I had another long visit from the Rev Mr Barrett… he went through my pictures again… for I had not sold any pictures since the single one on the day of the Private View. When in our round we had reached the Monograms, he astonished me exceedingly by saying that he would like me to do his.

"Oh! But do you know it will be twenty guineas? 'Indeed I do… and I also know that they have a value far beyond what any money can compensate for.'"

There is certainly a sense in Georgiana Houghton's paintings that she created them before their time. Surrealist Automatism did not appear until thirty to forty years later, with attempts at changing the rules of art. Impressionism arrived with a 'less life than experience' attitude towards painting.

We have seen that the artists who instigated this first mediumistic automatism genre of spirit art had a good deal of difficulty being accepted. The next chapter considers an artist who created a 'higher form of automatism', one that saw the medium in trance, completely possessed or overshadowed by the spirit of a deceased artist. David Duguid was one of the few such artists in the nineteenth century, with the ability to create small oil paintings in dark séance conditions.

3

Late Nineteenth Century Trance Art

Whilst Victorian mediumistic automatism remained largely unrecognised by the formal art world, spirit artists continued to experiment with invisible communicators, with supernatural forces and mystical energies, in order to develop their unique canon of art further. These pioneers did not create art for the art world, but to demonstrate their conviction that invisible energies and etheric beings could make marks on paper or canvas, illustrating the principle that intelligent life existed beyond death and could be verified by their paintings and drawings.

These artworks were acknowledged by spiritualists alone. What did this matter if the art produced by spiritual techniques was of interest only to believers and followers? The artists' experiences while experimenting with spirit energies, art materials and séance conditions, strengthened their belief in life after death and rendered their interest in acceptance by the art world less important. A positive effect was that their work advanced Spiritualism's knowledge of spirit phenomena as they created their art. Between the mid-1850s and the end of the century, these persuasions resulted in a new art form, our second spirit art classification, as trance art emerged out of mediumistic automatism.

The production of trance art has a similarity with mediumistic automatism in that it involves an 'adjustment' of the medium's consciousness, to allow a discarnate entity to overshadow the medium and trigger the brain into the action of drawing – rather as a puppet would be controlled by the puppeteer. But for trance art the medium would be completely in a passive state, as though asleep. Any thoughts resulting in actions that appear to come from the medium were believed to originate from an overshadowing spirit.

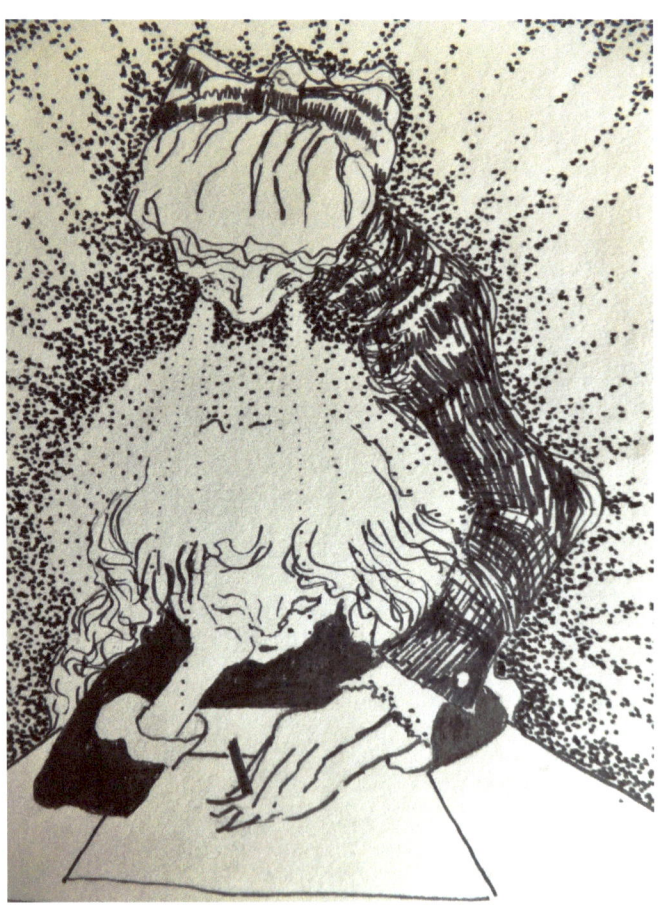

The Artist Overshadowed

These actions required a form of supernatural control of the medium's body by a spirit. It will help if we first frame the unusual cognitive conditions that were required during the production of spirit trance art. Although those involved in Spiritualism may already be convinced of these notions and understand their mystical complexities, some readers may not have experienced any spiritual or supernatural phenomena and will not be aware of the nature of spiritual symbiosis. The method of being controlled by the spirit of one deceased has been described as though the medium were 'a hollow bone with light winds running through it'. So it may be helpful to offer an explanation of how mediumistic automatism progressed into trance art, in the hands of the main instigator, the medium David Duguid (1832-1907).

David created small oil-painted miniature landscapes during séances in Glasgow towards the end of the nineteenth century. He believed his guiding spirit to be a seventeenth century landscape painter, Jacob Isaakszoon van Ruysdael (c.1628-1682). The medium offered his body as a host in order for this artist-in-spirit to create paintings by complete possession and control.

The altered state of consciousness known as 'trance' was becoming well known during that century; there were essentially two states of the phenomenon, the partial or overshadowed state and that of complete control. The latter involves the medium consenting that an often unknown spirit personality might fully manipulate their physical body, often rendering him or her entirely unconscious. However, in order to create trance art, for example, a slight adjustment to the medium's motor skills was required – a conscious action by the host to alter their state of mind from being able to see, hear and sense the physical world around them, to one of dissociation from the physical body. This would permit the hand of the medium to be moved without their will.

In the 1840s, the entrancement of mediums was initially induced using a form of hypnosis known as 'mesmerism', invented by the German scientist Franz Friedrich Anton Mesmer

(1734-1815). This enabled a medium to succumb completely to the supernatural energies of what they believed to be their spirit guide. Spoken or written words would then be allowed to flow through his or her mind, believed to come directly from a deceased spirit. This process was considered completely normal and the watchers or listeners would regard it with complete reverence.

Simply put, trance speaking is about the submission of the medium's thinking self to a disembodied mind and allowing that mind to speak through the medium's voice box. The practice of trance speaking was the forerunner to trance art. The first spiritualist medium to use trance speaking as a tool for the spirit world was Andrew Jackson Davis (1826-1910), the so-called 'father of modern Spiritualism'. He explained in his autobiography[23] that in 1841, seven years before the inauguration of Spiritualism, he fell into a deep state of mesmerically-induced trance. In this condition, similar to a deep sleep, he began uttering sentences about healing, medicine and matters seemingly unknown to him as a young and uneducated farm labourer. The trance state appeared to affect his consciousness because he was no longer thinking or speaking as himself: the words used, the tone of voice and the rhythm and metre of the voice were changed.

Davis came to believe that the scientist and philosopher Emanuel Swedenborg (1688-1772) was speaking through him. Moreover, he seemed to gain advanced academic knowledge similar to that of a medical doctor, with an ability to diagnose illness and predict future health conditions. As his expertise grew, he also predicted the coming of Spiritualism several years in advance. A result of his trance speaking and healing was that the practice of mesmerism became fashionable with American and British spiritualists who wished to develop their mediumship into trance states

---

[23] *The Magic Staff: An Autobiography of Andrew Jackson Davis* (J S Brown & Co,1857, reprinted by Lulu.com 2017)

of consciousness, forming a willing synergy with those deceased souls whom they accepted as their spirit guides.

There is a photograph taken of a trance medium by American photographer Shannon Taggart during a New York séance.[24] As an art-form it reflects the notion of a movement of consciousness, as the medium's thoughts transcend her physical body to allow a disembodied consciousness to enter. The medium's recollection was one of serenity: her own thoughts were extremely clear as another's thoughts spoke through her. Whilst this account could appear to suggest that two personalities are present within the one body, it can be understood as similar to two separate intelligences within one room, the one listening as the other spoke. Once the secondary consciousness of the spirit had finished, it withdrew – rather like an external hard drive or memory stick being disconnected – leaving the medium's physical body and mind completely intact and unharmed.

Psychologist David Fontana (1934-2010), in what he told me was his "life's work"[25], explained this form of supraconscious mediumistic trance state of mind in this way:

"In the course of [mental mediumship] the medium may go into a trance-like state, in which to all intents and purposes consciousness is lost and the spirit communicators speak through her, or she may remain conscious and simply relay messages as she receives them. Sometimes she may, either in trance or consciousness, use automatic writing i.e. allowing communicators to control her hand and write their messages."

In his study of mediumship and altered states of consciousness, Fontana thus defined the process of trance, describing it as though the entranced medium may or may not lose consciousness while writing (or, as we shall see, drawing). Frederic Myers went further in questioning the processes of the trance state, maintaining that the voice

---

[24] *Shannon Taggart: Séance* (A Fischer, T Oursler, Fulgur Press, 2019)
[25] *Is there an Afterlife?* (D Fontana, O Books, 2005)

or drawings produced could be created by any one of several means: the medium's subliminal mind, their supraliminal self, or their own incarnate spirit communicating with discarnate spirits, who relay sensate impressions to the spirit medium in order to speak, write or draw.

"Possession, to define it for a moment in the narrowest way, is a more developed form of Motor Automatism. The difference broadly is, that in Possession the automatist's own personality does for the time altogether disappear, while there is a more or less complete substitution of personality; writing or speech being given by a spirit through the entranced organism."

There is still lack of academic clarity as to the shift that happens to the medium in trance. The spiritualist belief is that the external consciousness of a discarnate spirit has the ability to dominate, or at least influence, the medium's actions or speech while their physical body is in a light or deep trance. This is shown in my illustration, inspired by my own experience of the trance state while drawing a spirit portrait, which shows the 'overshadowing' of a medium by a spirit guide. Trance art requires the artist-medium partially or completely to lose consciousness during control by a spirit.

It is worth noting that spiritualists do not refer to this state as 'possession' because it is believed that there is a coming together of two minds, the medium's being passive and accepting the control of the spirit guide so that they may work through the medium's physical body. For mediums like Davis or Duguid, a partial or full trance state of consciousness would have been required for their trance speaking, writing or painting. This bridge between the two worlds of life and death is symbiotic.

Of course, modern Psychology recognises that not all who hear – or appear to use – others' voices are mediums. The genuine spirit medium is trained to give evidential messages concerning those who are communicating with them. Nonetheless, and despite the science of Psychology being new in itself, there were those who made it their mission to try and discredit any medium. The proper investigation of paranormal phenomena became important.

According to Frank Podmore (1856-1910), a medium could be tested for the genuineness of the trance by the lack of movement or "insensibility of the conjunctiva" (part of the eyelid) which, he maintained, cannot be faked[26]. This test entailed a member of the séance to examine the skin over the eye for movement during the trance state. Podmore came to believe that David Duguid was really entranced because he was fully examined before, during and after his trance painting sessions.

Citing one of the first spirit writing automatists, James Garth Wilkinson (1812-1899), Podmore also described automatism as "spirit writing" or "spirit outflow", defending it "on the grounds that, whether proceeding from the subject's own deeper nature [i.e. the medium's own spirit] or from external sources [i.e. a deceased spirit], the guiding power was alike spiritual." Yet he struggled with theories regarding any supernatural processes used in the making of trance art, whilst accepting it for what it was. He admitted that "existing psychological theories [are] inadequate to explain the phenomena in full" – the viewer had to trust the medium as well as the method. Spirit artists maintain that they consciously reposition the mind from its natural state and become passive to the deceased.

A contemporary medium has claimed that a 'spirit communicator' would completely control them in order to paint through their body, as David did.[27] Thus the result becomes their truth: the spirits must be drawing the images through them. This conviction was crucial both to the medium and to those who sat with them in the séance room and this truth was especially important for Duguid, as the sitters reinforced his belief in his painting methods after the séance.

---

[26] *Modern Spiritualism. A History and a Criticism* (F Podmore, Methuen & Co, 1902)
[27] *The Link: Extraordinary Gifts of a Teenage Psychic* (M Manning, Colin Smythe Ltd, 1974)

Throughout history there have been few trance mediums, perhaps indicating that it is an exceptional ability to maintain an unconscious state of mind while submitting to the control of a spirit guide. In particular, the processes involved in the making of trance art require a deeper consciousness, making this different to that of the mediumistic automatism of Anna Mary Howitt and Georgiana Houghton and thus a new classification of spirit art.

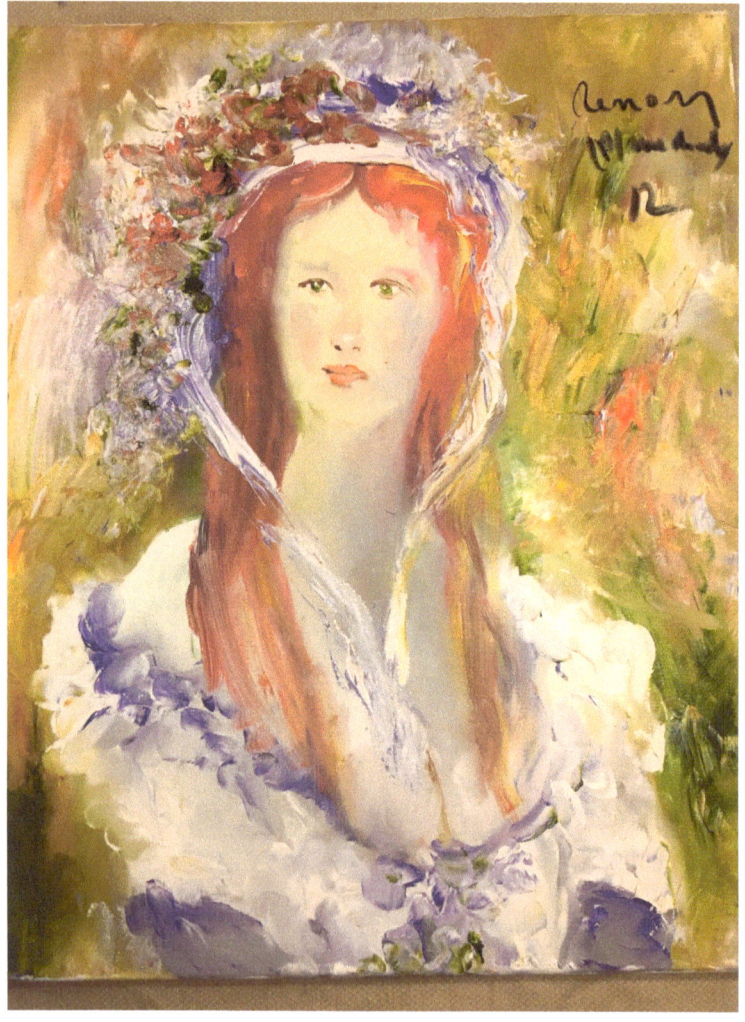

Ida

There are contemporary trance artists, such as the Brazilians José Medrado (see *Ida*, 'after Renoir') and Luiz Gasparetto, who demonstrate mediumistic art in daylight and in front of an audience while in an altered state of consciousness. *Ida* was created in full light on a canvas laid flat on a table in front of an audience. Also on the table were tubes of oil paint and differently sized brushes. The medium went into a full trance while standing at the table, picked up paint and spread it onto the canvas. To finish the work, he signed with the overshadowing artist's signature.

But David Duguid was the first and most well-known of the Victorian era. He was born into an ordinary working family in Dunfermline and trained as a cabinet-maker, only experiencing the world of Spirit from 1866 when he was in his early thirties. This took the form of ghostly impressions that manifested as visions in the form of spectres and then as raps on furniture.

Realising that he required help to understand what was happening to him, he attended his first séance in that year at the house of Mr H Nisbet, a publisher, where he first experienced table-tilting and the movement of objects around the room. Those who witnessed these events recognised him as a natural medium. Able to write automatically and with a propensity towards drawing alongside his automated texts, Nisbet suggested that David attend a course at the Glasgow School of Art.

He trained in drawing there for only four months and by 1872 was painting images in oils during Nisbet's trance séances, working in this way and as a 'direct-drawing' medium until his death in 1907. (Direct-drawing was an American term describing the phenomenon of a spirit drawing directly onto paper or slate without human interference. It is different to trance art, where the medium holds the pencil or brush, and will be discussed in Part Two of this book where it is named Psychographic Art.)

In Britain during the latter part of the nineteenth century, mediums who wished to develop an ability to be controlled by spirit were usually chosen by a group of spiritualists and invited to join their undercover séances. This custom was because it was felt legally dangerous to demonstrate mediumship due to the Witchcraft Act of 1542 and the Vagrancy Act of 1824, which forbade "fortune telling" and "conjuration of spirits". (This law was only repealed in Britain in 1952.)

Duguid challenged this law by continuing to practise until his death. Once a member of a séance, he quickly revealed his ability for communication with, and trance-control by, the spirit world. And it was through this exposure to deceased spirits in a Glasgow séance room that he further developed the ability to create trance art. Responding to the spirit messages communicated to him, his art evolved into three forms: automatism, trance and direct drawing and painting. He was one of only a very few recorded trance artists in spirit art history.

At first, and shortly after beginning to attend Nisbet's séances, he produced drawings while in a mediumistic state of partial trance only. The trance art began unexpectedly after Nisbet's daughter, who could write automatically, placed her hand lightly over David's in order to promote the automatic action of writing and, later, drawing. Oil-painted landscapes began to appear in 1865, when his hand started to tremble, firstly producing small insignificant marks on paper.

Witness statements by Nisbet and the other séance sitters indicated that he developed this regular state of shaking or trembling of the hand, something that often occurs when mediums draw their first such art. Both Anna Mary Howitt and Georgiana Houghton had created automated art regularly by the time Duguid began his spirit art journey, but they do not seem to have developed further into the trance, direct or psychographic forms of spirit art as he did.

It was unfortunate that David's early paintings appeared to resemble the work of deceased artists so accurately that some thought them to be copies of the others' pictures. Frank Podmore suggested that they were from Cassell's *Art Treasure Exhibitor* (c.1870). His séance companions, however, observed that he presented himself differently while in trance, assuming that he was being controlled by a spirit guide and that this artist was creating the images. The Dutch painter and etcher, Jacob Isaackszoon van Ruisdael (1628-82), and the figurative painter Jan Havickszoon Steen (1626-1679), have been cited by the séance sitters as the originators of his paintings and drawings. As an entranced artist-medium, he was believed to have been controlled by each of these deceased artists, one at a time, yet he himself was unaware of them.

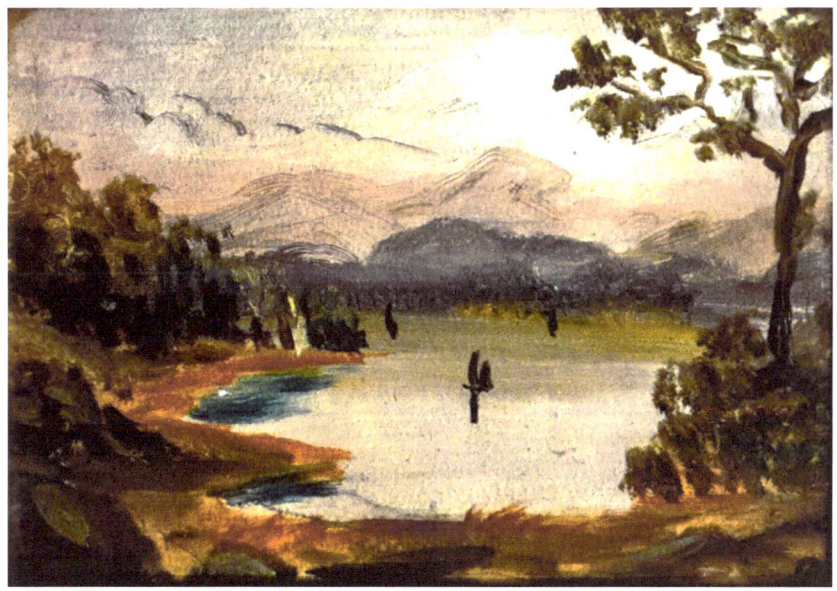

Untitled ('The Pool')

All artist-mediums have their own individual styles. David Duguid was able to recreate impressions of previously painted scenes, leading critics wanting an explanation of how he could be 'channelling' art that resembled the work of a deceased artist. Frank Podmore gave this description of the process:

"From Dr William Anderson, who witnessed the performance in 1866, and who had himself no doubt that the medium was really entranced, we have a fairly accurate description of what took place.

"For the convenience of the spectator, the easel was usually placed in full light of the gas. The medium, apparently in deep trance, and with his eyes apparently closed, would paint rapidly and effectively, the subjects being for the most part landscapes, lakes, waterfalls, etc… [W]hen the light was reduced to a feeble glimmer and a screen held between that glimmer and the canvas, the medium in Dr Anderson's presence went on working at the picture, introducing, during the most complete darkness, several small boats on the surface of the lake."

This was a description of the supernatural events that occurred when the small oil painting *Untitled* (here referred to as *The Pool*) was painted in December 1872. This work is now housed at the Arthur Findlay College, Stansted Hall in England and is one of the few works produced by David left in existence. It is known that the painting was created over several sessions, both in the séance room and in David's home; so the methods used in its creation were not always witnessed, leaving him open to questions regarding its authenticity. Alongside the postcard-sized painting, however, is a handwritten caption on a small piece of cardboard referring to witnesses, the method and the outcome of the oil painting, which helps us to understand the medium's approach:

"This picture has been painted by Mr David Duguid, in a state of trance, first in the house of the subscriber, and afterwards in his own house in Glasgow. Mr D professes to be under the direction of Jacob Ruisdael, a Dutch painter of the 17th century, who has also directed him in the same condition to paint other pictures, some of them reproductions of his original works.

"In this and other paintings the medium Mr Duguid paints in trance – that is, with his eyes firmly closed, and apparently unconscious of those who are witnessing, or of things taking place around him while in that condition. The abnormal state of Mr D has been repeatedly tested by putting out the light while he was engaged in painting to the entire stupefaction of the visitors. The picture was begun in the house of the subscriber on 5th Feb. 1869, in the presence of Mr A Kennedy, and Messrs Ninian John Stuart (of Stuart and McDonald), and was continued from that date to be worked on for about three or four months at intervals of a week and finished in the medium's own house in additional sittings.

"At these sittings, there were present as witnesses, amongst many others, the following: Mrs H McBeau, Trandensen Colnworks [sic], Mr A Glendinning, Port Glasgow, Mr Robt. Greig, Hillhead, & Angus Smith of Manchester, Mr J Adamson, 165 Cowadden, Glasgow, Harry Wheat, printer, 164 Forngate, Glasgow. Dec. 19th 1872." [sic]

This document supports a belief that there was no deception here. Whilst *The Pool* appears not to show the same expertise as that of Ruisdael, having been produced by an amateur artist, the witnesses claim that it was indeed created through David by the deceased artist.

Certainly, there are painterly differences between Ruisdael's paintings and Duguid's. Great expanses of sky and land are typically depicted in Ruisdael's landscape paintings, and David's *Untitled* (c.1872) demonstrates discrepancies between the compositional traits of the two artists. Ruisdael's image, when recreated by David, offers a poor depiction of nature, sky and cloud, without the aesthetically strong representational qualities of the deceased artist. These qualities present in his landscapes are what Ruisdael was famous for. His illustration and sensitivity towards dramatic ethereal space and solid land mass are missing in David's reproduction; likewise, the voluminous clouds of his skyscapes do not have the same quality of form or sense and distance. *The Pool* also lacks the relevant artistic sensitivities, as does David's *Untitled* (here referred to as *The Castle*).

These differences present us with a conundrum. As a working artist myself, I can see that David Duguid's heavy, bold characteristics of land, water and sky in his mimetic landscape paintings, seem amateurish in comparison with Ruisdael. It is as though an inexperienced student had copied the master's work, using the experience to improve his own style. An art historian might well say that there is no comparison between their styles in terms of competence.

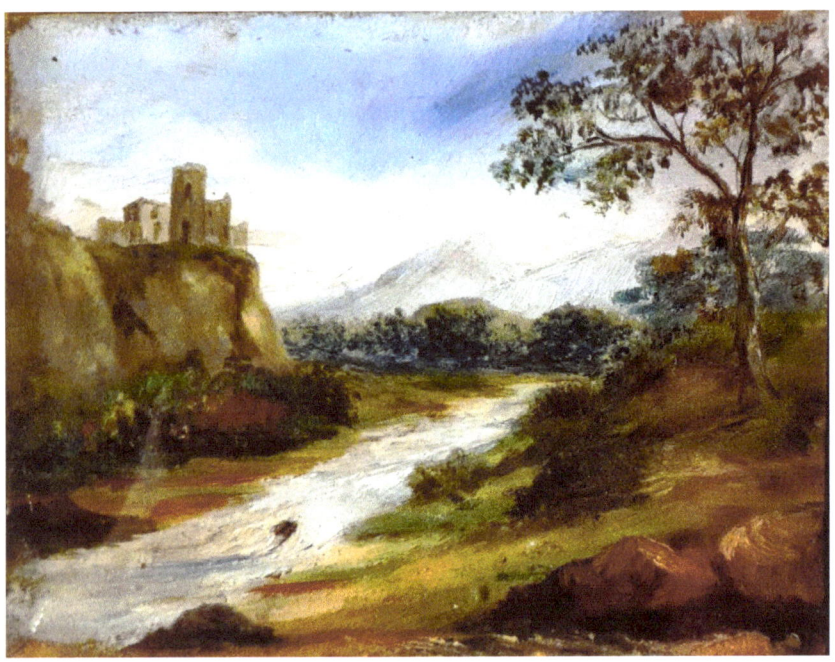

Untitled ('The Castle')

The issue here seems to revolve around whether the believed-to-be controlling spirit artist told the séance circle (in a spirit message) that he was Ruisdael, so the sitters believed it to be true. And Duguid was acclaimed at first by Frederick Myers and Frank Podmore as a proficient spirit artist. Well, whilst spiritualists might believe the works shown here to be painted by Ruisdael because the medium's body was possessed by him, the law would define the images as Duguid's since he was holding the paintbrush. And in another brush with law, it should be noted that David was later charged with fraud, for bringing ready-made paintings to a séance in Manchester in April, 1905, at the age of seventy-three.

His work was further distrusted when he began to produce a form of 'direct drawing' whereby an image was said to have been created without the use of a physical hand at all, a process that preceded psychographic art (our third classification of spirit art). Direct drawings were believed to be created by discarnate spirits directly onto the art surface, using the psychic energy of the medium rather than their physical hand.

This atmosphere of disbelief was only exacerbated by critics of spirit art, such as Harry Houdini (1874-1926), demanding proof – not just that the paintings were accurate representations of a deceased artist's work – that the postcard-sized images had not been copied in advance and then secreted in trouser pockets into darkened séance rooms. As a consequence of all this, David Duguid stopped creating spirit art completely shortly before his death.

Although his spirit trance paintings and drawings were interesting as artworks, they are unlike any other classic art forms and remain an enigma in the history of art. This makes the art unique as well as complex. But although it can be seen that our first two classifications of mediumistic automatism and trance art might possibly replicate a deceased artist's style, the quality of the art – the painterly merit of the mark-making, colour choices and composition – appears poor and offers little to the collector or curator as saleable or viewable work.

An interesting and different slant on the work of a trance artist is offered by the thought-provoking *Thompson-Gifford Case* of 1907. This concerned the well-known New England landscape painter, Robert Swain Gifford (1840-1905) and a New York goldsmith, Frederic L Thompson. The latter began to create drawings while apparently in trance and controlled by Gifford, some six months after the artist's death. This was despite Thompson being on record as saying that he "despised" Spiritualism.

An especially illuminating element of the case is whether, in the opinion of various commentators, it is one of 'possession' or of 'obsession'. Psychiatrist Dr Graham Kidd has suggested it is conceivable that spirit artists create artworks similar in style to those of the deceased, but that the impressions may not actually come from the deceased.[28] In other words, the drawings are created by the artist and not by any supernatural method (and whether or not the artist believes in life after death).

Kidd argues that the work might originate by means of existing "visual and sensual templates" i.e. muscle memories built up from childhood and accessed later in life. Even though a non-artist says they "cannot draw", in their subconscious mind there should be experiences from earlier life when they did draw and thus memories that the mind can call on later. Moreover, citing the Thompson–Gifford case, he maintains that because Thompson had already viewed some of Gifford's work there were also visual memory imprints in his mind.

The basic facts of the case are these. Robert Swain Gifford died in 1905, leaving his stormy drawings and paintings, as part of an exhibition, to the American Art Association of which he was a member. Frederic L Thompson did actually view these paintings, realising that he had met Gifford more than once in the marshes of New Bedford, Massachusetts, in 1902, while out hunting. Gifford had been sketching there. In the summer of 1905, Thompson began seeing insistent visions in his mind and was "…suddenly and inexplicably seized with an impulse to sketch and paint pictures", beginning to draw as though in a trance state and despite having had no interest in or experience of art before this. In particular, he had 'hallucinations' of trees and landscapes that he associated with Gifford, and reported that he felt his mind being taken over by the artist. There were drawings very similar to Gifford's, especially of the island at Nonquitt, Massachusetts, where Gifford had a summer house.

Early the next year, Thompson went to the Gifford AAA exhibition, not knowing that the artist had in fact died. While there, he

---

[28] Society for Psychical Research, London: lecture entitled *The Mind Behind the Hand: Transmitted Art, Music and Literature* (April, 2011)

reported that a 'spirit voice' in his ear invited him to "take up and finish my work."[29] Thereafter, Thompson produced a number of paintings of artistic merit and was even able to sell some, although he didn't disclose their origin; indeed, an art critic told him that one of his pieces resembled Gifford's work. Thompson was particularly haunted by a vision of some gnarled oak trees and felt compelled to find the scene; eventually, following up information from spiritualist mediums and Gifford's widow, he found the exact trees on the island of Nashawena, one of the Elizabeth Islands, a place he had never been to. It had been Gifford's "favourite place". There are many other intriguing aspects of this case.

Gifford's and Thompson's drawings are remarkably similar, and there was a suspicion that Thompson had copied them. The spiritualist viewpoint sides with the notion that he was inspired by the artist from the spirit world. Kidd, however, is clear in his view that Thompson had viewed Gifford sketching but may not consciously have remembered the scene.

Spiritualist mediums have undergone considerable investigation; the Fox sisters and the trial of Helen Duncan are notable examples. On this point, Harvey Irwin and Caroline Watt have said:

"Parapsychologists [need to be] alert to the stratagems of fraudulent mediums… on the other hand, it must be acknowledged that while Spiritualism perpetuated psychical research and posed many questions for researchers to pursue, investigation of mediums have failed to authenticate any parapsychological phenomenon."[30]

But spirit art has not undergone the same thorough research and there is little information either to defend its philosophies or to

---

[29] In 1907, Thompson asked James Hyslop, a university teacher of Philosophy and psychical researcher, to investigate the matter. His report was published as *Contact with the Other World* (J H Hyslop, The Century Co, New York, 1919)

[30] *An Introduction to Parapsychology*. (H J Irwin, C A Watt, McFarland and Co, 5th ed. 2007)

disagree with them. Whilst Kidd considered that automatism and trance art may unwittingly be a product of a medium unknowingly using muscle memory, and the influence of deceased artists, Irwin and Watt suggest that there is just no real answer to any claims of paranormal authenticity. Myers would agree.

Trance artists such as David Duguid and Frederic Thompson believed that they had famous artists working on their paintings or drawings with them. In David's case there is written evidence from the séance sitters indicating that, while he held the brush and mixed the paint, Ruisdael painted the images. Yet the art produced is, in the main, of such indifferent aesthetic and painterly quality that it seems naïve in comparison with the work of those who were believed to have painted through them. In view of this, it is challenging for some to believe that spirit art has been created by deceased master painters. In his later years, David's integrity was dashed by investigators and psychologists.

How to summarise the methods of mediumistic automatism and trance art? We can say that the drawings and paintings were created by the living artist's own hand, while under the inspiration, or persuasion, of other-worldly spirits. Trance art perpetuates spiritualist belief that the deceased may not only control the living, they can also create art by using the body of a willing subject. There has never been any suggestion that these mediums were subjugated to the will of the deceased, rather that they agreed to be controlled.

This form of art was, and still is, created in the context of 'mental mediumship', meaning that the mind of the medium becomes taken over by the mind of a spirit. Our next chapter explores the technique of 'physical mediumship', where the creation of drawings and paintings involves no use of the human body at all.

These classifications of spirit art are called 'psychographic drawing' and 'precipitated painting', and involve supernatural power alone, invisible energies created (it is believed) by the spirits of the deceased alongside a physical medium who acted as a 'powerhouse' but whose hand is not involved.

PART TWO

PHYSICAL MEDIUMSHIP

Portrait and Figurative Painting

FOREWORD

As mediums began to understand how the energies of the spirit world worked, spirit art began to change. Whilst mediumistic automatism and trance art were created through the brain and hand of the medium, less and less of their physicality was used for the next two classifications of spirit art. Psychographic drawings and precipitated paintings were produced using energy alone, the physical hand not being necessary in the creation of fine art and drawings.

Of course, image-making was traditionally done in the Victorian era by artists using brushes, paints and pencils. So artwork produced by chalks, pencil leads and dust particles being manipulated on slate, board and canvas by invisible energies was almost literally unbelievable, despite being produced directly in front of witnesses.

It certainly caused consternation for those who did not believe in an afterlife. The creators of the work, Fred Evans and Henry Slade, the Bangs sisters and the Campbell brothers, were much examined by investigators – and occasionally thought of as fraudulent.

To begin to understand what was happening, we need to recognise that a specific type of supernatural energy had to be available. Only a certain type of medium has this energy as part of their natural human make-up, and a physical medium needs to be present in the séance room in order to make available the specific supernatural energy that can conjoin (it is believed) with the actions of the deceased.

Other physical phenomena associated with physical mediumship are rappings (such as happened at Hydesville), the movement of objects or dust (known as telekinesis or teleportation) and the production of objects out of thin air (called apports). The most common types of phenomena during the making of psychographic drawings and precipitated paintings were the transportation of dust and fibres across a room, painterly apports and the movement of small slivers of chalk or graphite on chalk boards or slate.

Physical mediumship was often produced in the dark and many psychographic drawings could not be seen as they were made but only heard, as the materials wrote or drew on covered slates. Naturally, this encouraged some psychic investigators in their belief that there was cheating going on. Because of this, slate drawings and precipitated paintings were then mostly produced in the light of lamps, or in daylight, sometimes watched by hundreds of people in American meeting rooms as they 'developed like a photograph' on the board or canvas.

Despite scepticism, these beautiful artworks were collectable by spiritualists and many are now housed in two spiritualist centres, Camp Chesterfield in Indiana and the Lily Dale Assembly in New York, with curators very happy to speak about them.

I have personally found these paintings and drawings extraordinary and worth travelling across the globe to see and discuss at first hand. In the following chapters I try to offer a balanced approach, using testimonials and the artists' own thoughts in books and articles from the time the works were created, and the expertise of the curators. I also give my own descriptions, as an artist, of how the art was created, the materials used and the beautiful surface quality of these exquisite works, whilst discussing the roles of medium and investigator.

The author T A Bland described the creation of a different and special form of spirit art, a 'precipitated painting':

"Suddenly, many in the audience lead [leaned] forward in their chairs, sitting rigidly, their eyes tensed and fixed on the canvas, from which a thin, vapour-like cloud, or shadow it seems, sweep across it, pulsates and then flickers out. After a few more tense moments, shades of definite colour begin to appear, as if successive layers of fine dust have been thrown or precipitated on to the canvas."[31]

This writer coined the name 'precipitated painting' when attending a later demonstration of spirit-created art in 1911, the first time the term had been used to explain this unique method. As with psychographic art, the viewer was presented with portraits seemingly produced by unseen supernormal energies, without the medium having any knowledge of the subject depicted. But moreover, the paintings were believed to have been created without any human assistance save for the paranormal energies built up by a physical medium, who merely had to be present during the emergence of an image.

We can now only imagine the excitement in the meeting rooms where these paintings were created. Bit by bit, and untouched by human hand, a clear painting board would be filled with colour that eventually emerged as a portrait or a flower painting, rather like a photograph developing. With their belief in life beyond death, spiritualists naturally believed that discarnate spirits were responsible for the paintings by manipulating dust and fine fibres from the environment; others, of course, simply could not believe this.

The phenomenon suggests that the medium who produced the energy to generate the painting was less a creative artist and more a 'facilitator' enabling the art to be made. The artists, supposedly, were spirits of the dead.

As an art concept, the use of unearthly physical phenomena distinguishes precipitated painting from other spirit art classifications, as it does from conventional art. As a working artist myself, I suggest that the process is a little like blowing pastel dust onto

---

[31] *In the Celestial World* (T A Bland, T A Bland & Co, 1905)

the surface of paper or canvas that has a layer of glue on it so that the dust sticks to it. As different colours fall, the initial shades will change; if the pastelesque colours and process of precipitation are controlled by some 'intelligence', then the images become well defined.

Whilst spiritualists believed they knew how this form of art was made, the methods involved in the practice were not easily understood by outsiders. I have said that the production seems to mimic that of a photograph developing. However, the paintings were produced in colour from 1892, before the advent of colour photography, so it is unlikely that they were created using any sort of photographic material on the painting surface (which is not to say that there were no other means of production available).

Sceptics such as the clergyman Reverend Andrew T Osborne and the psychic investigator Hereward Carrington remained unconvinced, but other prominent Victorians such as the writer Sir Arthur Conan Doyle and William Usborne Moore, Vice Admiral to Queen Victoria, were sure that the spirit world alone made the paintings. Doyle asserted that precipitated paintings were not created at all by the hands of the mediums but produced using supernatural energy alone. Others, such as Harry Boddington, described the supernatural procedures and physical phenomena as relying on "psychic matter" that consisted of "psychic structures", "fleecy clouds" and "balls of light"; these could materialise and dematerialise, lift and transport large and small objects, including the dust the paintings were made from, between rooms.

It seems that only two pairs of mediums had the innate prerequisite supernatural energies to facilitate the creation of these paintings, between the years of 1892 and 1920. These were the Bangs sisters, Mary (May) (1862-1917) and Elizabeth (Lizzie) (1859-1920) Bangs from Chicago, and the Campbell 'brothers' Allan Campbell (1833-1919) and Charles Shourds (d.1926) who lived at Lily Dale, New York. They were not trained artists but each developed paranormal abilities from childhood, in particular the supernatural trait of physical mediumship. The precipitative process was an anomaly in art and also psychically rare, unique to Spiritualism and mostly defined by these four mediums.

4

Psychographic Art, Slate Writing and Portraiture

Spiritualist writer Harry Boddington described the methods of creating psychographic writing in this way: "Direct writing is sometimes called psychography. Automatic writing may be transformed into 'direct' writing if sufficient physical power is present. Paper and pencil are simply laid upon the floor or the table and messages are received without perceptible human aid."[32]

He believed that a spirit could create art when devoid of a physical body. From this philosophy and practice, a spiritualist theory was formed that the human spirit was capable of communicating with the living in many different and extraordinary ways after the death of the body. This chapter is therefore about the process by which objects, such as a piece of chalk on slate or pencil on paper, could be moved without living human intervention in order to create a picture. This was how psychographic art was made.

---

[32] *University of Spiritualism* (H Boddington, Psychic Book Club, 1946, reprinted Psychic Press Ltd, 2002)

Although I have witnessed the movement of objects on a séance table, I have not myself experienced drawings created between slates. It seems that this form of spirit art required a huge amount of psychic energy that could manifest ectoplasm. In my own book *Portraits from Spirit* (2011), I describe the appearance of ectoplasm during a physical séance as an "etheric… pulsating light" and an experience never to be forgotten. There was a metallic taste to the air as the intense 'light show' developed, while the sitters hardly blinked not wishing to miss sight of the spirit performance that followed. We can only imagine what the Victorian sitters made of the appearance of lights, objects, movements and rappings in the séance room and the heart-pounding excitement that ensued.

We now understand that the first two classifications of spirit art – automatism and trance – used a supernatural method of *triggering the brain* to move the hand of the medium during the making of the art. But psychographic art did not require use of the medium's physical body as such, only their energy. This energy is believed to have been produced entirely from an invisible supernatural source, a unique form of energy created by both the medium and a disembodied spirit, which enabled production of ectoplasm. David Fontana referred to ectoplasm as "a semi-physical material which may derive from the vivifying energy body said to permeate the physical body [in life] and leave it at death." So, according to both psychologist and spiritualist, this invisible ectoplasm is a living substance that can move objects including chalk on slate.

The paranormal creation of images by the use of ectoplasm is called a physical phenomenon and the medium, as energy facilitator for producing this ectoplasm and then the art, is known as a physical medium. There are photographs from a contemporary photographic exhibition in *The Perfect Medium: Photography and the Occult* showing such mediumship. It looks perhaps like strings of cheesecloth are emanating from the mouths or other orifices of mediums, usually women who are completely bound and tied to chairs so that they could not free themselves.[33] This supernatural ectoplasm seems to have been vital to the formation of spirit writing, the drawings on slate and the creation of precipitated paintings.

It was in fact quite a normal thing for writers and artists to attend Victorian séances in order to watch paintings appear on a board, slate or canvas by this method and without the use of a living artist. In Britain this was a form of entertainment as well as a religious practice, although mediumship was illegal so these events were often held behind locked doors in secret venues. Writer and spiritualist Sir Arthur Conan Doyle expressed his feelings about psychographic impressions on slates that were produced during séances he attended, saying that, "Slate writing mediumship is a remarkable manifestation."[34]

Unfortunately, of course, due to the invisible supernormal procedures – the making process could not physically be seen – it was difficult to verify that the psychographic images were actually created by a so-called spirit. This caused problems regarding authentication and so séances began to be held in lit rooms to try to prevent any suspicions of fraud.

Indeed, Harry Boddington wrote of the séances he witnessed with one of the first psychographic mediums, Henry Slade, remarking that they "…were held in broad daylight. Slates were usually cleaned by investigators who often brought their own, and some people retained the wrappings around them while the writing was going on, or brought locked and sealed folding slates which did not leave their hands until after the séance." These precautions softened the idea of trickery or of meddling with the drawing surface before the séance began, particularly for Henry

---

[33] *The Perfect Medium: Photography and the Occult* (C Cheroux, A Fischer, Yale University Press, 2004)
[34] *The History of Spiritualism, Vol. 2* (A Doyle, reprinted by The Spiritual Truth Press, 1989)

Slade's mediumship. Doyle also wrote about his scrutiny of the procedure during séances. However, this did not stop psychic investigator Ray Lancaster attempting to discredit Slade's working methods.

There were two pre-eminent artists who facilitated these pictorial impressions on slate and who were known as 'direct writing' or 'direct drawing' mediums. The first, as mentioned, was Henry Slade and the second was Fred Evans. My information on just how these unique spirit-drawn chalk and graphite drawings between slates were produced has been obtained from autobiographies and biographical testimonies transcribed by observers, and from writer Ron Nagy, the curator of the Lily Dale Museum where some slate drawings are housed.

Psychographic drawings were produced throughout the second half of the nineteenth century and into the beginning of the twentieth century, predominately in America and Britain. Physical mediums produced an invisible vitality that could move a piece of chalk or graphite between locked and/or bound slates. In order for this unearthly, non-solid, etheric manifestation to occur, the medium required an innate ability to create ectoplasm. This substance cannot be produced by any medium: they either have the propensity towards its creation or not. Spiritualists say that physical mediums are born with this ability and that it cannot otherwise be developed.

The process of psychographic drawing begins, it is said, when energy from the spirit world becomes conjoined with the medium's energy. These two forces double in strength and are substantial enough to be able to move objects within the surroundings of the medium – a phenomenon known as telekinesis. It was reported by Victorian mediums and sitters in 'physical circles' that, by manipulation of this energy, objects as big as tables and grand pianos were lifted up and moved around the room without living human assistance. Flowers, coal and cloths such as handkerchiefs would appear out of thin air or be translocated through walls or floors between rooms.

It was also found that this form of mediumship could be used to create writing, diagrams and drawings, generated without the use of a living human hand. These are psychographic and precipitated drawings and paintings, which have little creative relationship to automatism or trance art by virtue of the differences in their production.

For these two new forms of art to be created, the job of the medium was to lay out art materials ready to be engaged by the supernatural energies surrounding them and to offer their personal, inherent spiritual energy. The mind of the medium would not be employed during the process, rather their psychic energy: they did not physically create the art but were facilitators of it.

The ectoplasm produced by the mediums was found to be an 'etheric' substance with varying degrees of luminosity and opacity. Whilst not being physical, it could be formed into shapes including human body parts. There is a wax cast of a hand that was made from an ectoplasmic structure produced during a physical séance that remains on show at the Arthur Findlay College at Stansted Hall, UK.

Ectoplasm can be said to be similar in a sense to ice, in that it becomes an apparently solid form and then disappears as if by melting. It is fleeting and ostensibly non-existent, or non-physical. To have a wax model formed from it is very rare. My personal experience of ectoplasm is that it appeared as wisps of light, not solid or at all earthly, like smoke from a blown-out candle that can clearly be perceived by sitters in a completely dark room. In another séance it manifested as a thicker substance that moulded into shapes with the appearance of a hologram. It is difficult to touch because it recoils from physical objects or as hands reach towards it.

Strangely, these mystical wisps gradually form shapes that do not cast shadows. Yet they can be seen in the darkest of dark rooms, as would be a florescent object. Although I have not myself witnessed the formation of solid structures like the sculptured hand mentioned, I have observed objects move, splash, bang or scratch like the claws of a dog on a door, as well as strands growing into wispy etheric structures that built up into three-dimensional shapes only to disappear as though returning back to its origin.

Ectoplasmic substances growing from the orifices of a medium were reported to have been photographed by Victorians such as Baron Albert von Schrenck Notzing (1862-1929) during physical séances.[35] For example, this supernatural material can be seen as strands of a cheesecloth-type substance, emanating from the nipples of a female medium, which was then reported to build up into figures.

There are many expressions of physical phenomena: independent voices, paranormal lights and noises, the independent movement of objects (telekinesis) and the materialisation of spirit forms or objects (apports). So, if solid things could be transported around a room without physical help, a conviction grew that a piece of chalk or graphite could draw on paper or slate, manipulated by deceased spirits using supernatural energies. Furthermore, the transport of dust from fibres, of paint particles or oil pigments from different parts of a séance-room, could manifest spirit art. This method of drawing and painting is, naturally, unique to Spiritualism and unrecognised by the conventional art world.

In America and Britain, the facilitators of this artistic process were 'spirit-mediums' rather than the hands-on 'artist-mediums' described earlier. According to Ron Nagy, curator of the Lily Dale Assembly museum in New York State, they worked by "aiding the mystical forces present in the séance rooms, conjoining their psychic powers with the energies from the spirit entities." These

---

[35] *Phenomena of Materialisation* (A v S Notzing, Kegan Paul, Trench, Trubner & Co Ltd, 1923, reprinted by Wildhern Press, 2008)

ideas thrived and were rapidly advanced by experimenting with what were believed to be the energies of spirit beings.

Paranormal investigators such as Hereward Carrington (1880-1958) considered the whole thing implausible, but despite such investigation there was little evidence of fraud in the actions of these mediums. There were at times, possibly, aspects of deception in the making of psychographic art, but this was not enough to prevent two new classifications of spirit art from being produced over several years. Spiritualists remained convinced that psychographic drawings and precipitated paintings were created by spirits of the deceased. Indeed, there was a positive effect on people outside the movement, validated by the large numbers who attended demonstrations of precipitated art produced in theatres and community centres in late nineteenth century America.

When I visited Ron Nagy, a contemporary expert in the history and creation of psychographic art, he described the psychographic method in the words of a woman who had obtained a drawing from Pierre L O A Keeler (b.1855), a nineteenth century psychographic slate writer:

"I brought my own slates. They were tied with my own ribbon. I put them on the table in Keeler's home on Cottage Row. He sat across from me. It was in the daytime; the room was really bright. He had his hands on the table. Then he and I placed our hands on those slates. I heard a light scratching sound and he said, 'It's done.' The message was for me, and something personal that no-one else would have known about." The woman gave a clear testimony of her experience and appeared to be in no doubt that she would receive a message from a discarnate soul. This message was special and intimate to her and her description gave credence to the actions of the medium.

How was it done – did a miniature spirit hand appear between the slates and scratch out a message? Nagy commented that at the time there was such strong belief in the afterlife as a real world, some thought that the spirits of children were able to draw using minute pieces of chalk on slate by means of supernatural energies.

Alternatively, invisible energies created by physical mediumship in combination with forces built up inside the séance room have never been – and probably cannot be – proven nor disproven.

There was certainly no suggestion in the account above of any fakery or fraudulence during the time the artist made the portrait. Whilst psychic investigators such as Carrington and the Seybert Commission of the University of Pennsylvania, in 1884–1887, tried to dismiss the phenomenon, they were unable to conclusively argue either way. On the other hand, some mediums claiming similar abilities were caught out: Francis Ward Monck (b.1842), a Baptist minister who later became a spiritualist, was exposed in 1876 by a sitter, an amateur magician, was convicted and served three months in prison.[36]

The psychographic art of Fred Evans and the writing of Henry Slade demonstrate a distinct style in each medium's work, both supernaturally and artistically. The mediums relied on a symbiosis between themselves and the spirit world as they gave up their energies to whomever (or whatever) moved the mark-making tool between two tightly bound slates.

Henry Slade was acclaimed by respected spiritualists such as William Stanton Moses, the Nobel Prize winner Lord Rayleigh and the writer Sir Arthur Conan Doyle. Yet he too suffered accusations of deception and fraud for his psychographic works towards the end of the nineteenth century, notably by Sir Edwin Ray Lankester, a British zoologist. Despite being rigorously tested, however, he was acquitted and acclaimed by others although his work remained 'suspect'.

Whilst there were other mediums like Slade who produced the required supernatural energy to create psychographic art, such as

---

[36] The conviction was quashed on technical grounds in 1877 and a subsequent court case in 1907 partially restored Monck's reputation. Always a controversial figure, *The Banner of Light* said of him, "He became pious, it is said, and the Church took him in – or, perhaps, he took the Church in."

Pierre Keeler, they were predominately 'direct writing' mediums and did not obtain drawings. Indeed, direct drawing onto slate was quite rare and Fred Evans was one of the few spiritualists who had this innate supernatural ability to create recognisable impressions of deceased people in chalk on slate, or graphite on board. Let us look more closely at these two important individuals.

Henry Slade (1835-1905)

Born at Johnson's Creek, Niagara County in the USA, Henry Slade became one of the most well-known direct writing mediums of the late nineteenth century, working in Britain and Europe from 1876. *London World* described him in that year as "…highly-wrought, nervous temperament, a dreamy, mystical face, regular features, eyes luminous with expression, a rather sad smile, and a certain melancholy grace of manner, were the impressions conveyed by the tall, lithe figure introduced to me as Dr Slade."

The Seybert Commission Report of 1888 also described him as "…probably six feet in height, with a figure of unusual symmetry… his face would attract notice anywhere for its uncommon beauty [as] a noteworthy man in every respect."

Henry was known for his physical mediumship. At one time early in his development he "…stood five feet from a table and caused it to tip over by a wave of his hand and raise an organ from the floor by five feet or more."[37] These were incredible feats so it was not long before he was invited to Britain, where there was a great deal of interest in physical mediumship. Once in London, Henry was tested for his mediumship at every demonstration and it is said that he was able to produce ectoplasmic sculptural forms similar to the hand mentioned earlier.

In these early days, Slade was highly respected as a great medium with *The Spiritualist* describing him as "one of the most remarkable

---

[37] *Slate Writing: Invisible Intelligence* (R Nagy, Galde Press Inc, 2012).

mediums in modern times", capable of taking the place of the most famous medium of the nineteenth century, Daniel Dunglas Home. He was known to have been very business-like, collecting twenty shillings a time for his sittings, the fee and set-up of his meetings being his own choice and not that of a manager. He had only one sitter at a time, with séances conducted both in the light or the dark and taking approximately 15-20 minutes. These were quick sittings! He had no hesitation and was decisive. As an example, one of his first séances in Britain was with the editor of *The Spiritualist*, W H Harrison; it took place in strong sunlight at a table on which Henry Slade simply placed a small piece of pencil onto a slate.

During this period, investigation of psychic phenomena was rife and became an accepted integral part of spiritualist life because there was perceived to be a requirement to provide proof that the human spirit survived death. It was thought that the images should provide evidence that what the mediums were producing was accurate. As time passed, Slade had certain difficulties with creating legitimate scripts through the process of slate writing and physical mediumship, and was accused of fraud. Psychographic drawings were examined thoroughly by the Seybert Commission because there were people like Harry Houdini who tried to prove that what Slade did was mere trickery: the results were not definitive.

He continued to create psychographic writing until close to his death but the opinions of fakery lingered. However, spiritualists continued to visit him for slate writing and drawing. For no known reason, the kind of work that he and other psychographic artists produced have never been replicated since the deaths of those who created them.

Fred Evans (1862-c.1930)

Frederick P Evans was a major creator of psychographic chalk drawings on slate and his work clearly identifies the methods by which this classification of spirit art was produced, a style that was challenging to find fault with. Whilst few mediums had the supernatural ability to produce the ectoplasmic energy required, Fred's work was so closely documented that fraud seemed impossible.[38] A vivid account of his life and work is given by James Owen.[39]

Evans was born in Liverpool, England, in 1862, the great-grandson of the Welsh social reformer Robert Owen. Like the Hydesville Fox sisters he showed mediumistic tendencies from childhood. At the age of thirteen he became a sailor, boarded a merchant ship and went to sea. He was believed to have had a charmed life, surviving being swept overboard and then back onto the ship by the same wave. He also almost drowned in a shipwreck off Cape Horn as an apprentice sailor, but was recorded to have been a brave and fearless man.

On separate occasions he saved the lives of three people. Once, when ashore in Liverpool, he saved a woman from drowning as she was pushed overboard from a ferry in the River Mersey. Later, on two other separate occasions, he prevented two labourers from drowning in the Liverpool docks. In 1881 he was awarded two pounds by the Liverpool Shipwreck and Humane Society for his bravery. After being shipwrecked again in 1884, Evans made his home in San Francisco and began his study of Spiritualism; his psychographic writing and drawing began the next year, with an ability to create these works in complete darkness.

There is no record of him ever attending an art school or having any natural ability to draw. From records in the Liverpool Sailing Museum it is known that seamen with time on their hands during long voyages would often take up creative hobbies such as knitting or sewing 'woollies' and 'silkies', or inscribing tattoos on other sailors' bodies. Whilst there is no record of him taking up

---

[38] In 1898, the magician Chung Ling Soo claimed to have revealed the 'fraudulent slate-writing methods' that Evans, Slade and others had used.

[39] *Psychography: Marvellous Manifestations of Psychic Power Given through the Mediumship of Fred P Evans known as the Independent Slate Writer* (J J Owen, Hicks-Judd Company, 1893; reprinted by HardPress Pub)

such crafts, it is true that some of his artworks closely resemble the tattoos that sailors created on their long journeys.

There is a description in his own writings, quoted by Owen, of one of his first experiences of supernatural activity and psychographic drawing:

"I sat in my darkened room holding my slates [a pair of 5" x 7" school slates] for about half an hour each evening for two months, and never received a manifestation. I began to get discouraged, and determined that I should sit no longer for development [of physical mediumship], so I put my slates away and retired.

"I had been in bed about three minutes when I could see a bright luminous light at the foot of my bed. I thought it might be caused by the light creeping through the blinds and reflecting on the white door knob which was opposite the foot of my bed… several luminous lights were seen floating at the foot of my bed. Some would be about the size of a dollar and others would be about the size of a man's hand… In holding the slates I felt the slates as though I were holding onto a small battery.

"I then began to hear distinct raps on the slates, and a few nights later I realised that [the spirits] were manipulating the crumbs of pencil I had placed between the slates… I found a small number of small marks on the slates… [I]n February 1885… I devoted myself to the exercise of my mediumship as an independent slate-writer."

He went on to explain that he himself required evidence that his experiences were truthful and not imaginary before he would accept that the spirit world had created the images found between the slates. This indicates that when he first began his work as a medium he did not accept all that he experienced as direct communication from the spirits of the dead. As his mediumship developed, drawings were produced by placing the secured slates between his hands or apart from his body on a table or chair so that his hands could be seen a distance away from the slate. He did this so it could not be inferred by observers that he meddled with the slates during séances.

His drawings were distinctive female portraits produced by slivers of white chalk between two grey-black schoolroom slates bound together and then placed between the hands of the sitter. This would often be in daylight. The sitter would sometimes sense vibrations from between the slates as writing or images were produced. The image, often created in just two minutes, would represent someone deceased and known to the sitter.

Within four years of starting to create psychographic drawings he was invited to Australia. Writing in *Queensland Figaro and Punch* in October 1888, an unnamed reporter seeking spirit communication wrote:

"It must clearly be understood that, although I cannot consider the conditions of the above séance incontestable and as not being explainable by the most ordinary means of parlor [sic] conjuring… my mind is still perfectly open and receptive through impression."[40] The reporter was clearly moved by Fred's actions during the fully lit séance, yet expressed some concern regarding the methods he used while creating the drawings.

Despite this unease regarding his art works, his biographer James Owen provided a description of the circumstances around the creation of one of Evans' most evidential pieces, *Spirit Josephine* (c.1886). This portrait has been signed by 'St Clair' whom Fred believed to be his artist-in-spirit, a deceased artist who drew the portrait in chalk between two slates by using supernatural energy manifested through Fred's physical mediumship.

"Josephine first made her presence known to us while we were sojourning in the city of New Orleans, during the winter of 1885-1886… The psychic [Evans] said that there was a beautiful young lady present who wished to send a message to [my] wife… 'Good evening, Brother James. I see that Mattie has gone for a little trip. But you know that I am very happy to see you have come here this evening. Mr Grey requests me to explain the meaning of the seven

---

[40] http://trove.nla.gov.au/ndp/del/page/8760316?zoomLevel=3

stars that you see in my hair represented in this picture. Well I will tell you I belong to a band of spirits who act as missionaries to aid and uplift the fallen and assist them to a higher sphere… All spirits belonging to this order wear a star, so that they are recognized when manifesting anywhere. I am glad you are both pleased with my picture… This from loving JOSEPHINE.'"

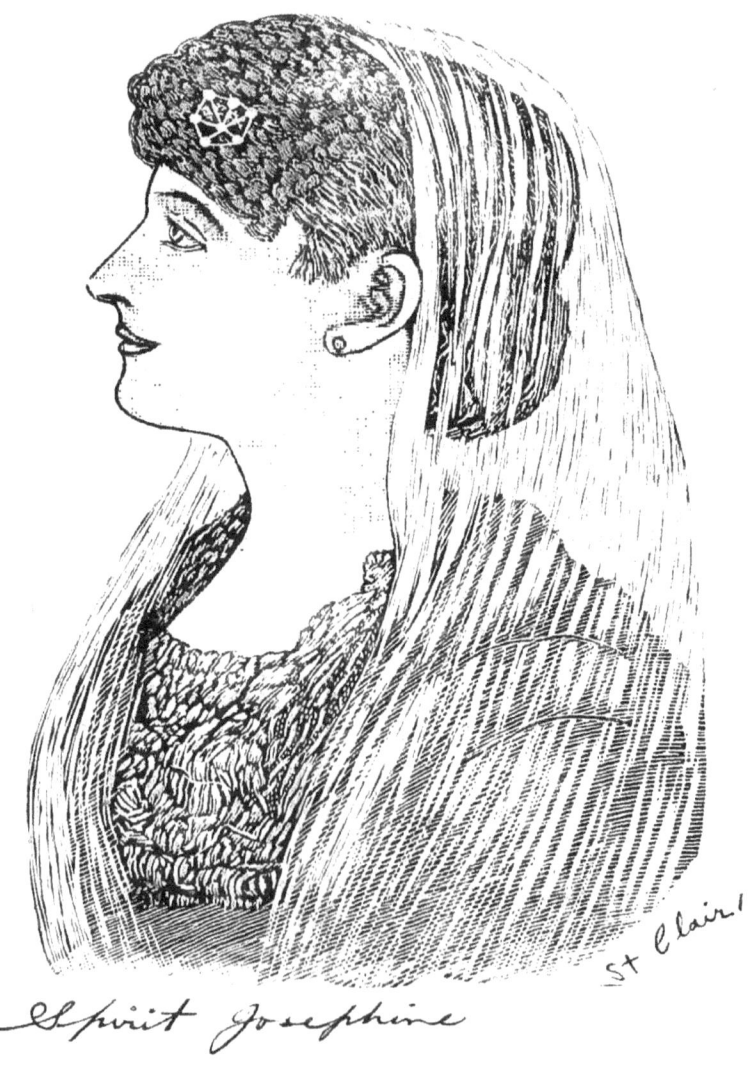

Spirit Josephine

Characteristic of most of the chalk-on-slate drawings, *Spirit Josephine* depicts a deceased person as they would look in life. Owen and his wife, who was present at the meeting and held the slates as the drawing was created, later confirmed that the image was a portrait of the wife's deceased sister. Verification of the identity of a spirit often rests within the context of the drawing and the elements within the image, so this recognition fulfilled the proof that Evans needed to ensure that he was creating a truthful image on the slate as evidence of life after death.

For nineteenth-century sailors, tattoos indelibly scratched onto the body gave comfort as reminders of home while away. Many favourite tattoos were illustrations of family members, whilst stars and birds were visual superstitions representing omens. In particular, stars represented a superstition that the ship they sailed on would return home safely and, if not, their bodies would be recognised by their tattoos. A two-tone star was pivotal to mapmaking and was often drawn onto nautical maps and compasses, becoming a symbol for a seafaring man's direction in life. As a sailor, Fred Evans would have been familiar with tattoos scored onto the skin of his fellow shipmates on long voyages and he may have learned the skills of tattooing himself. It is clear from an artistic point of view that his drawing has qualities reminiscent of maritime art.

Josephine's drawing is depicted with a seven-pointed star in her hair. The heptagram is an ancient pagan symbol of magical power, and is also suggestive of the seven planets of classical astrology from which sailors took their bearing and direction in life.

Looking again at Josephine's star there is a story emerging that may be reminiscent of Evans' maritime life. The drawing mimics his familiarity with seafaring knowledge as her hair reflects her passage from the mortal world to her spiritual life. Added to the picture on the slate are the words, "…stars designates the zeal and development we [spirits] have made in our particular work." The words suggest that the stars relate to a higher or lower state of spirituality for the deceased in the realms of spirit.

Fred, a world-travelled sailor for almost ten years, would have understood the meaning of the spirit impressions in this image. The psychographic drawing of Josephine also contains elements such as hairstyle and facial shape and profile very similar to common seafarer tattoos. So is it possible that the psychographic chalk images were subliminally drawn by Evans, mimicking sailors' tattoos, rather than by the spirit St Clair? Biographer James Owen dismisses this notion, saying:

"As to the fact of the picture being produced by independent spirit power, we simply *know* it to be true. Of course there are those who think we are the victims of deception. We cannot blame them. These modern revelations of psychic power are too much for the unschooled comprehension."

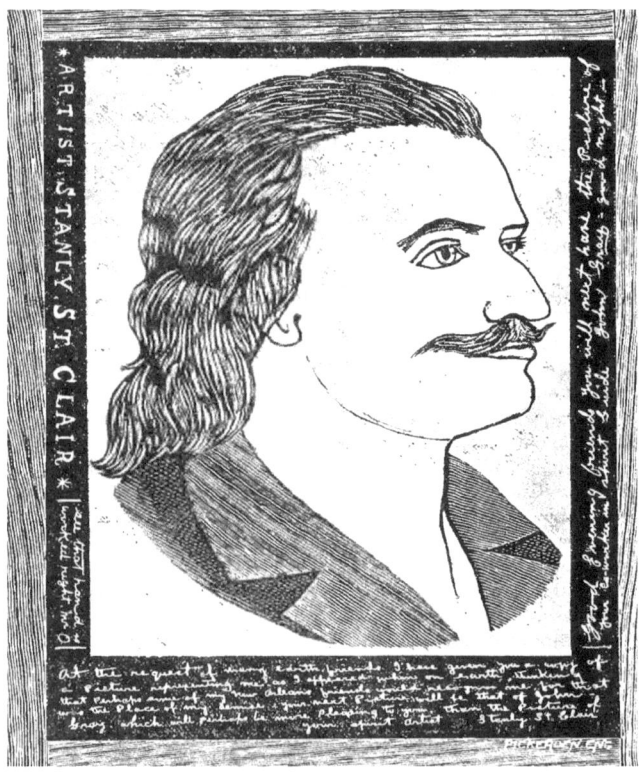

Our Spirit Artist

The pen and ink drawing *Our Spirit Artist* illustrates the actual slate image that would have been created originally in negative form (white on black). The image represents 'the artist in Spirit', Stanley St Clair, reportedly sketched by himself through Fred Evans' mediumship on the inner surface of one of a pair of slates held in the hands of Mr and Mrs J J Owen.

Although photography was already in vogue when Fred Evans' psychographic chalk drawings were being created, there is now no photographic evidence to identify the person drawn on the slate. The recipients of these drawings relied on their own memories of the deceased for recognition, which means that the images might or might not have been good likenesses of their deceased loved ones. Nonetheless, his chalk drawings were accepted as honest and truthful and the recipients believed that they were drawn by spirits from the afterlife. However, as more mediums attempted to create psychographic drawings on paper and slate, more investigators attempted to prove them duplicitous.

Spiritualist beliefs were important to the creative processes of psychographic art and to the spirit-mediums who created it. This and the next classification, precipitated painting, were produced using supernatural powers alone. The facilitating physical mediums, influenced by what they experienced in the séance rooms, were convinced that post-mortem spirit portraits were generated by paranormal forces conjoined with their own spiritual energies, and not by artists. Of course, some people outside Spiritualism did not agree that the dead could create art in combination with the living.

Devalued by the art establishments in England, spirit art in America during the latter part of the nineteenth century did not associate itself with the culture and society of academic art. Spirit art had no great commercial value but was more of a means to an end, a tool for believing that one could converse with the sacred or the deceased; it was only valued by those who believed that the spirits could create art. Major artists, on the other hand, would need to keep their reputation and cultural collateral intact in order to sell their work (an issue that caused James Whistler to sue critic John Ruskin for libel following a scathing review).

The next chapter examines the fourth classification of spirit art, precipitated painting, an art form produced using similar methods of physical mediumship and the supernatural phenomenon of joining one's energies with those of the dead. Unfortunately, investigations of trickery became routine to the makers of precipitated painting, although the art itself would later become a convincing element of belief in life after death.

5
Precipitated Portrait Painting

Precipitated paintings were produced by means of an extremely unusual – and unbelievable to some – paranormal method. We should therefore try to find an explanation of the painting processes that were applied during the creation of such artworks. Whilst spiritualists and mediums who have trained in physical mediumship have their own understanding of the supernatural processes involved, it must be difficult for others to comprehend fully this extraordinary phenomenon of art produced without the use of the human hand.

We shall also explore separately the facilitation of precipitated paintings by two particular sets of mediums in order to illustrate the differences in their techniques. Accounts by those who observed the actualisation of the spirit images in real time should help to explain both the supernatural and artistic processes.

There has never been a complete survey on how many precipitated paintings were made and how many have survived since 1892; they were not recorded when produced and details have been lost over time. However, in America there are now two sites where many of the paintings are curated: the Lily Dale Assembly in New York State, and Camp Chesterfield, Indiana, where a small booklet by Irene Swann, *The Bangs Sisters and their Precipitated Portraits* (1969), was written.[41] Other paintings are privately owned or scattered worldwide, predominately in American or English spiritualist churches and centres such as the Portsmouth Temple of Spiritualism, UK, and in private homes. Where these paintings have survived, it is due to their owners' acknowledgment of the uniqueness and rarity of the artwork.

As curator of the Lily Dale Museum, a small and neatly painted clapperboard house in Library Street, Ron Nagy re-enacts the history of the place for visitors on tours. His books and talks describe the spirit and psyche of the place and its people, including investigators and doubters, and offer a steadfast texture of verbal folk accounts on how precipitated art was made. He passes on his knowledge and understanding in order to conserve spiritualist belief and the conviction that life exists beyond death.

Nagy contends that the technique of precipitation was produced in daylight so that everyone in the séance room could see what was happening, in order to provide proof that it was a supernatural process and there was no trickery. Nonetheless, a non-believing Reverend Stanley LeFevre Krebs (1864-1935), an American psychologist, proposed that a portrait had already been painted from a photograph and placed underneath a plain sheet of paper or canvas; then, because the painting was behind a curtain, the surface could be taken away to reveal a completed portrait appearing to have been painted by the spirits. Duplicitous activity was debated among other non-spiritualists. In 1901, Krebs attempted to provide proof of fraud at an evening demonstration with the Bangs sisters, but according to Nagy there was no conclusive outcome to this.

Still, the four mediums who facilitated the making of precipitated paintings were constantly barraged by questions regarding

---

[41] Published by Hett Memorial Art Gallery and Museum, Camp Chesterfield

the veracity of their work. I don't feel it would be helpful to go into too much detail here regarding the authenticity of their methods because arguments about whether the artwork was or was not produced by supernatural energies and the spirits of the dead are on the one hand religious and philosophical and on the other hand irrelevant to the images as pieces of art. Proof for or against life after death is almost certainly impossible and it will be more valuable to analyse the aesthetic make-up of the paintings.

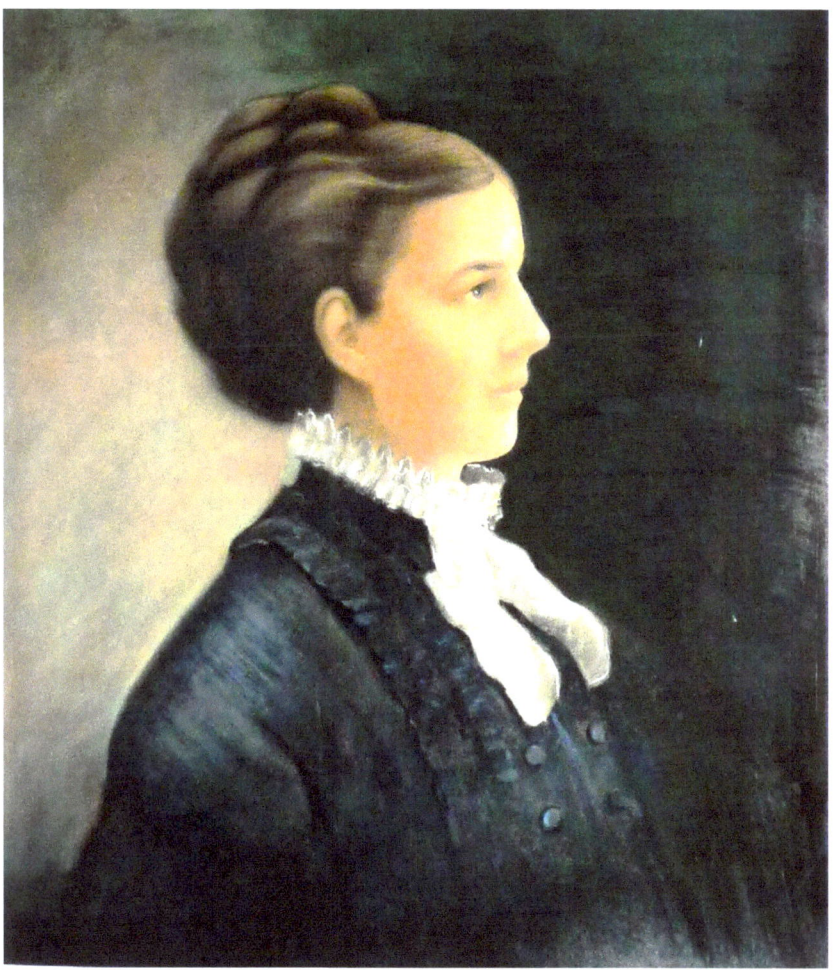

Iola

William Usborne Moore witnessed the production of a precipitated painting of his cousin, Iola. He testifies in his book *Glimpses of the Next State* (1911)[42] that, during the precipitation period, the image fluctuated as though an invisible artist were firstly sketching the portrait then filling in detailed parts such as the eyes or pieces of jewellery; this, he thought, provided the image with details of proof of the deceased. Nagy adds that, "In many cases, after the entire portrait was finished, the eyes gradually open, giving a lifelike appearance to the whole face." Despite others' doubts, we see that those who witnessed the making of precipitated art accepted credibility of the supernatural forces at work as they watched the paintings develop.

The painting of *Iola* was brought back to England and bequeathed to the Portsmouth Temple of Spiritualism (as it is now known) by Usborne Moore's widow.

Lily Dale, where many of the precipitated paintings were created, is approximately sixty miles from the Eastman Kodak Company in Rochester, New York, where Brownie cameras were produced in the mid- to late nineteenth century. In 1941, Kodak was asked to analyse the substance from which the Campbells' painting of *Lincoln* (c.1898) was made. According to Nagy, "The Eastman Kodak Company used all the technology at their disposal and could not ascertain what the paint medium was." He maintains that their report was an endorsement of spiritualist beliefs, though part of the report has since been lost. This is a great pity since the report would easily have found any chalk residue. What the paintings were created with remains an anomaly.

It is curious that these artefacts seem not to have been created from pastel or chalk since, according to my interview with Nagy in 2008, when a picture was taken from its frame in order to ascertain the material used to create the art, the picture "left no residue on the [covering] glass" which ordinary chalk pastels may

---

[42] Reprinted by White Crow Books (2011)

deposit. Similarly the image was also "still sticky to the touch" after over one hundred years in the frame.

Precipitated paintings were not created using airbrush techniques or any other known art methods. Indeed, the surface qualities of the paintings have been likened to "the dust on a butterfly's wing", a dust apparently dropped onto the working surface by supernatural action alone and not by human expertise. This was done, it is said, by transporting dust particles such as minute fibres from clothing, skin, furniture and other furnishings present in and around the séance room, which mixture would then be deposited onto the art surface by the spirits of the dead, using the collective energy of the working mediums. The make-up of the substance with which this pastelesque form of painting was made is indeed interesting since it looks like chalk pastel but has no dusty excess. Pastels are usually sprayed with a fixative to keep the colour in place. These paintings do not give the impression of that and yet the body of the painting has somehow been kept in place.

This is how Nagy describes the phenomenon of precipitated art being made by the Bangs sisters (a similar eye-witness account is given later). Firstly, a pot of paint mixed with many colours would be placed nearby, then:

"Initially two blank paper canvasses mounted on frames were placed face to face and standing on a table, leaning up against a window. The sitter would sit beside the table… The sisters would be on the other side of the table… and a blind pulled down to the tops [of the canvasses]… After a while shadows would appear on the translucent surface, as though an artist was doing preliminary sketches… When the canvasses were separated, there would be a beautiful portrait on one, with no smudges of paint on the other, still plain one…

"The medium is present, along with the sitter and observers. The séance was usually done by appointment but in many instances auditoriums were used and random numbers were drawn to pick a sitter who would be requesting a painting. The spirit entity whom the sitter is mentally requesting to 'come through' or appear on the canvas is usually unknown to the medium…

"[In this situation] The framed canvas is placed on an easel… and lightly held by the medium or mediums, one on each side… The pot of paint [containing several colours] is placed in front of or on the floor near the canvas… The sitter mentally visualises the loved one who has passed on into spirit life… Slowly, like a Polaroid develops, the painting begins to appear. It usually takes fifteen minutes to an hour for the precipitation process to be complete."

Irene Swann also reflects that these paintings are greasy and "stuck to the finger on being touched [and yet] leave no stain on the paper which closely covers the canvas." Whilst unable to touch the actual paintings, I myself observed that there are no finger or brush marks whatsoever on the beautiful images produced by the Bangs sisters and Campbell brothers. Yes, a trained pastel artist may use a cotton-tip or brush to smooth pastel onto the drawing surface; this process takes a long time yet many of the precipitated paintings were produced in less than twenty minutes. Similarly there are no brush marks on the surface of the Campbell brothers' large scale oil painting of *Azur the Helper*, which was produced in less than an hour (see Chapter Six).

Naturally, the very action of holding the painting surface to the light of a window (as Nagy describes above) meant that sceptical investigators could suggest that the surface was coated with some kind of photographic chemicals requiring light in order to develop. And not all who witnessed the making of some of the paintings believed that what they were seeing was the truth. The covering and uncovering of the painting was a cause for concern for some viewers since the precipitated process seemed to mimic photography: images emerging slowly on the art surface like the developing of a photograph. Given such an unusual supernatural process, these artworks were distrusted by Christian ministers and psychic investigators alike, the spirit mediums accused of trickery and tested many times. But fraud was never proved and they continued to create spirit portraits successfully until the early twentieth century.

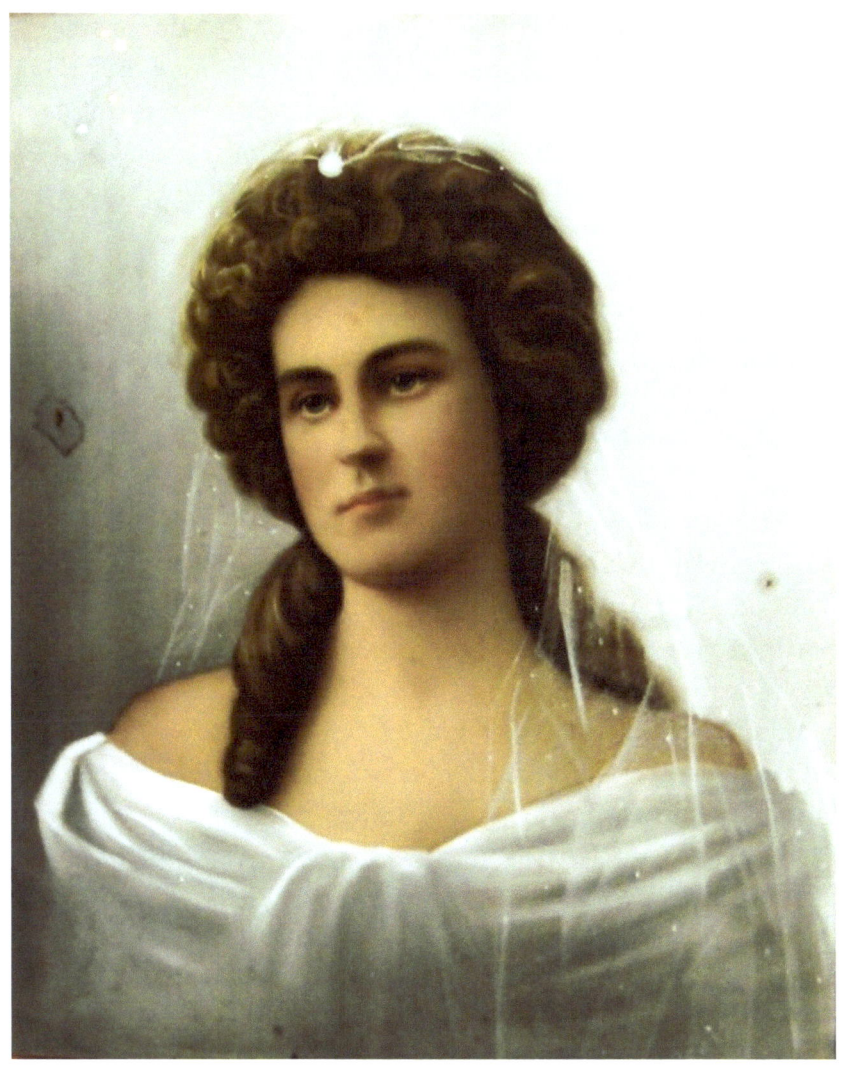

Pearl

My own first experience of a Bangs sisters painting was in Stafford, England, in 2005 when a member of the spiritualist church there told me that she owned a precipitated painting. This form of art was new to me but the lady knew I was a spirit artist and was keen for me to see the work, so I made arrangements to see the painting in her home. It was exhibited on a table easel together with a book about the woman portrayed.

I cannot truly express the sensation I had when faced with this portrait, named *Pearl*, because it was incredibly beautiful, as though emotion were radiating from it. Although it was approximately A1 in size with a plain golden frame, the size was not as noticeable as the energy that seemed to flow from it. I was overawed by the completely smooth texture, with definite pastel qualities, reminiscent of a Maurice de la Tour (1704-1788) pastel painting. This was my initiation into the extraordinary work of precipitated painting.

Both the Bangs sisters and the Campbell brothers continued to produce paintings until the death of their partners. There are subtle differences in their artworks and the two pairs of mediums facilitated the making of precipitated art in slightly different ways, but both maintained that they gave themselves and their psychic energy to the making of the art: they were not the artists but the energy behind the art.

This form of spirit art is not known to have been produced by any other artist or medium since the deaths of these four facilitating mediums; their supernatural methods and techniques have been lost and have never been replicated.

Mary (May) (1862-1917) and Elizabeth (Lizzie) (1859-1920) Bangs

The sisters Mary and Elizabeth were, it is thought, born in Chicago, USA, and were showing mediumistic abilities by the age of five. As they grew into adulthood they realised that their combined supernatural energies could transport objects such as coal from the ground to the ceiling and keep it up there, as well as move heavy furniture without physical touch.

Both sisters were married and divorced before the age of thirty, later moving back to Chicago to live with their mother. From there they travelled the USA, producing precipitated paintings publicly in theatres and halls and privately at personal sittings. The only residence they frequently returned to was their house in Library Street, Lily Dale, New York State, which they rented out while travelling.

According to American writer Eva Marie Garroutte, mediumship was relatively common in the homesteads of North America from the middle to the end of the nineteenth century.[43] From the 'burnt-over' district of the north-east, many immigrants arriving in the new lands for a new life sought spiritual security and so spiritualistic activity became commonplace. The first to be involved with this form of religious activity were of course the Fox girls, and it is likely that other child prodigies with a 'psycho-spiritual gift' developed their abilities through sitting with their parents and families in regular séances. This practice was relatively common in the nineteenth century; after the American civil war of 1861-65, many wanted confirmation that their loved ones had survived death.

May and Lizzie had begun creating precipitated paintings by 1892. Whilst they produced this art, they were not artists but physical mediums who could supernaturally generate ectoplasm and combine their joint paranormal energy in creating the pastel-like paintings. The 2004 exhibition *The Perfect Medium: Photography and the Occult* included photographs from the late nineteenth century that illustrate the production of ectoplasmic material and also show the mediums being tied up so that they could not be charged with fakery.

---

[43] *When Scientists Saw Ghosts and Why They Stopped: American Spiritualism in History* (E M Garroutte, in E Wuthnow (ed), *Vocabularies of Public Life*, Routledge, 1992)

Having heard that the sisters might be fraudulent, Vice Admiral William Usborne Moore travelled from England to Ohio to test them. In his book he describes the procedure and practices used for the production of a painting during his own sitting at one of their sunlit séances on the 20th January, 1909.

"Two thin canvasses were stretched on wooden frames and covered with thin paper and were placed face to face and held up to the window. The blind was drawn to the top of the canvasses and curtains hung up in my presence on either side. The window has a southern aspect, and the light coming in through the two semi-transparent canvasses is sufficient for the purposes of taking notes and seeing everything that goes on. The small oak table was lengthways in the window; the bottom of the canvasses rests upon it.

"May Bangs sat on my right side, facing me, and pinching together [with] her right hand one side of the canvasses. Lizzie Bangs on my left side, facing me and pinching together the other side of the canvasses with her left hand. I faced the middle of the canvasses, my nose being between two feet and two feet six inches from them. After a few minutes the canvas assumed various hues, rosy, blue and brown; it would become dark and light independently of the sun being clouded or not…

"Fifteen minutes after we sat in the window the face and bust appeared; the portrait was looking to the right, precisely the same aspect as it has now, framed, hanging in my room. Remember, I was looking through the back of the picture, and it was forming on the further side of that one of the two canvasses nearer to me; consequently, had it gone on as it was and been finished, it would now (when framed) be profile left. When the portrait was nearly finished the two canvasses were lowered towards me on to the table (mediums being impressed, apparently to do this)… the canvasses were separated and the finished picture put on the sofa in the next room, twenty-five minutes had elapsed."

From witnessing the production of this painting of *Iola*, Moore was convinced that the sisters, sitting with him over two sessions, had truly produced the portrait of his cousin by their supernatural energy.[44] He concisely reports that the painting was produced in front of him in daylight so that he could see whether or not it was created by human intervention, and he could find no deception. He also carefully archives how his precipitated painting appeared to fade in and out, giving the impression that an unseen artist's hand moved across the canvas, altering the image.

This is one of the very few known records of an account of such an image being created. Whilst there are common law statements held at the Lily Dale Assembly that precipitated images moved as the paintings were made, here we have a reputable statement by Usborne Moore that the portrait of his cousin changed as it was being created. This must have been a mystifying and never to be forgotten experience for this upstanding gentleman.

Incidentally, Moore reported that, in a later séance, Iola told him she hadn't realised she was dead until she saw someone cut off a lock of her hair from behind an ear. This event was unknown to the Vice Admiral, who had been serving abroad at the time, but on enquiry he found it to be true.

In Moore's experience there was no hoax or trickery involved in the Bangs sisters' work and this endeared them to him. He made sure that his photograph of *Iola* was kept very close to him in his breast pocket and he maintained that they were honest mediums, having travelled to Ohio to seek the truth. After this sitting he supported the sisters against an attacking article that appeared in *The Annals of Psychic Science* (c.1911) written by investigator and conjurer Hereward Carrington. Moore responded that the article was an "erroneous attack detailing fraud" and that "Many have

---

[44] As mentioned earlier, this portrait was later presented to the Portsmouth Temple of Spiritualism, UK, by Usborne Moore's widow. Some time after the Vice Admiral's passing, he manifested at a séance at which William G Gates was present and was asked if he approved of the portrait's position on the wall of the Temple. His reply was, "Slew it on the port side," where it could be seen to greater advantage. *The Secret of Death* (W G Gates, Psychic Book Club, 1944)

been the efforts to show that what happens in their [the Bangs sisters'] presence is the effect of pure conjuring on their own part. They have failed!"

However, the sisters' reputation was tarnished by the article and, although they created fewer paintings after Carrington's rebuke of their abilities, they continued to work and gain remuneration for their work. After May's death, Lizzie continued to paint until 1920.

The Bangs sisters' paintings were seemingly mesmerising during the creative process and also very beautiful and unique in the textural quality of the painting itself. Few have been found – some are in the Lily Dale Assembly Museum – and they are largely unknown in the art world.

Mentioned earlier is the precipitated portrait, *Pearl* (1905), which found its way to England and was later sold to a private buyer in Europe. Pearl is depicted as a young woman, illustrated as a veiled female figure set against a soft blue backdrop. The use of soft pastel shades in the painting seems to indicate the heavenly spirituality of the deceased. Finely pastelesque in texture, the velveteen portrait presents no obvious mark-making: it is devoid of finger marks, cross hatching or smudging. The surface appearance to the naked eye is astonishingly completely smooth.

Reading the painting as an artist, I see that the fine ethereal tones of grey, blue and ivory support the notion that the spirit of the deceased girl exists like this in the heavenly world of spirit. The colours mimic Renaissance holy art and the viewer is drawn to the eyes of this girl as though looking for a life beyond them.

T A Bland writes of the painting of Pearl as "taken [died] in her mid-teens" and notes that the painting was a perfect likeness of the young woman. He also reports on a public show at Camp Chesterfield, USA, by the Bangs sisters where he witnessed other precipitated paintings being created. Public demonstrations such as this would mostly consist of audiences of spiritualists who believed that the messages, writings and art were created by spirit entities. There were other times, however, such as during the Kansas City demonstration in August, 1911, when the sisters were heckled.

The purpose of these paintings was to provide evidence of the spiritualist philosophy that 'the taken' still exist but in another form. Pearl's wistful look – gazing as though deep in thought past the left shoulder of the spectator, almost a tear in her eye – offers the viewer a moment to ponder on the life that the deceased could have had. The hair lightly veiled in white voile together with the veil and the use of ethereal colours is suggestive of a marriage between Heaven and Earth, an immanence.

These paintings are unique in spirit art and very rare. I have been very fortunate to have met two very fine American mediums at the Arthur Findlay College, Stansted, England. These were Lauren Thibodaux and Susan Barnes, both with homes at that time in Lily Dale where many of the paintings are housed. I became a good team friend of Lauren's when we were working towards our teaching certificate in mediumship and I also met Susan during a course at the College. Both were kind enough to invite me into their homes to study the paintings as preparation for this book.

Each and every painting I encountered left me in awe of the technical quality of these works of art. Firstly, the surface quality was so finely executed it was impossible to believe that they had not been created by a human hand; secondly, the comment "dust on a butterfly's wing" does not really do justice to the fine coloured powder merged together on the art board.

For example, the painting *Clara*, believed to have been created under the mediumship of the Bangs sisters, clearly demonstrates a particular style and accuracy of their type of portraiture. Resembling popular American folk art (usually painted by itinerant artists travelling through American states) this painting is startlingly different from other Bangs sisters' paintings in that it is very clear and hard-edged in style and colour. The face and eyes are particularly captivating.

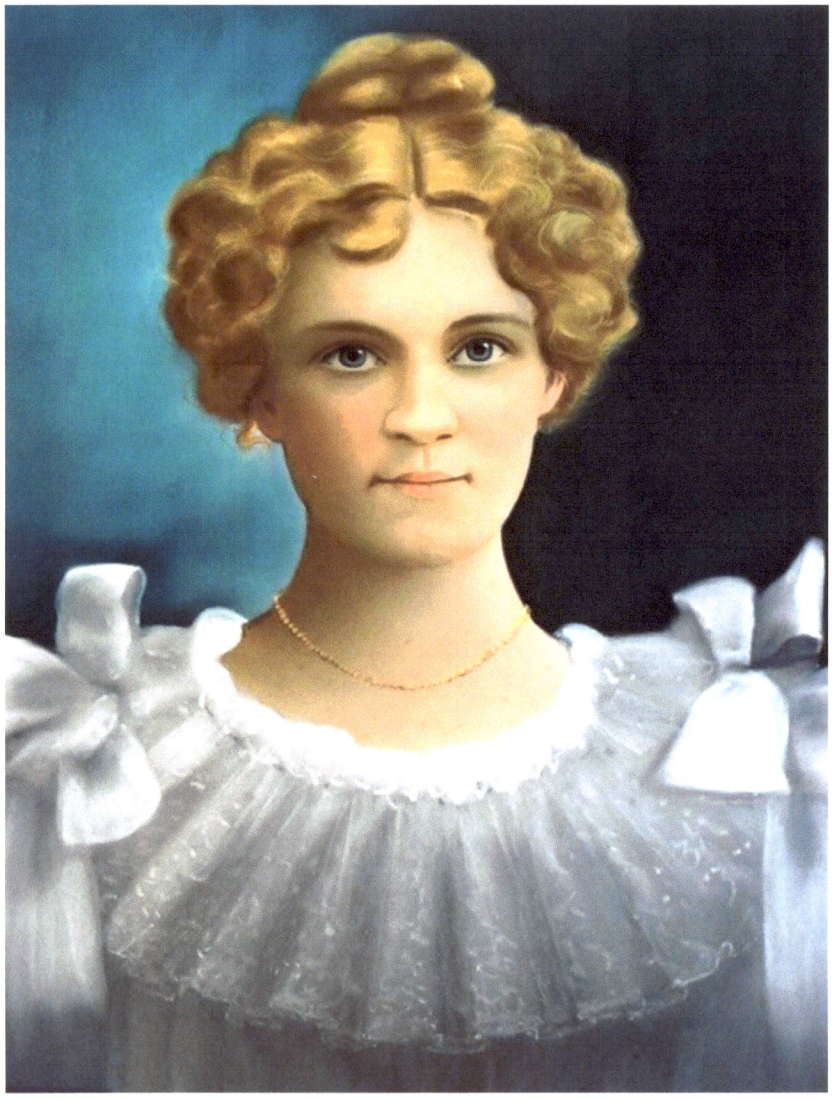

Clara

As Ron Nagy described the process of precipitation earlier, firstly a pot of paint mixed with many colours would be placed on or near the table where the mediums worked; then individual colours appeared to come out of the pot and separate as they were applied to the canvas. Yet *Clara* is less pastelesque and more oil painting in its surface quality. Moreover, the eyes are clear and defiant, very unlike the other examples of their work shown here. It has been suggested that the science of iridology can identify illness, and perhaps even cause of death, but Clara's eyes appear very alive and penetrating.

There is still a mystery as to quite how these works were created, not least because of the rarity of the events and of first-hand, eye-witness accounts. My understanding and belief, from the writings of others such as Nagy, Swann, Bland and Usborne Moore, is that the spirit world utilised the physical energies of the mediums to transpose dust and/or fabric particles from the surrounding rooms together with molecules taken from pastels or paints left in the séance room, in order to manifest an image onto a canvas or board. The image would appear on the art surface in daylight or by gaslight in full sight of the sitter or audience. Crucially, *it would even appear to change during its production*, such as the portrait looking left or right, having jewellery appear and disappear or change into another style.

But the exact materials which make up the painting are still unknown. There may have been oil or watercolour paint available (acrylic wasn't available then) whilst the Campbells' paintings look more like ceramic or oil paint. A Bangs' image such as *Pearl* looks like a normal nineteenth century American folk art pastel painting, whereas the Campbells' painting of *Azur the Helper* is typical of an oil painting on canvas. Each has a character of its own displaying the 'soul' of the once living subject.

I remember being in a physical séance a few years ago and was splashed with water! How can one explain that? Where did the water come from? Precipitated art is akin to that.

I have attempted to recreate the impression of *Pearl* myself, on the equivalent paper to Victorian Bristol board, but found that when laid down by hand the pastel did not give as smooth a quality as the original. Even trying to drop or blow the pastel dust onto the working surface was difficult, since the image was not easy to determine and it would float away wherever the air took it. Moreover, while sitting with others in séance conditions in the period 2015-17, with pastel dust in the centre of the circle, we had no success with any movement of the art material. I came to the conclusion that there needed to be a very powerful physical medium, or mediums, to produce this type of artwork now.

After 1912 there was a slowing down of the rate at which precipitated paintings were produced by the Bangs sisters at Camp Chesterfield and Lily Dale. There may have been two reasons for this. Firstly, perhaps, there was less interest in the work of mediums as the numbers attending spiritualist churches in the USA diminished; secondly, although the sisters had great acclaim within Spiritualism, their mediumship had been placed in doubt by sceptics. From records kept at Camp Chesterfield, one of the last portraits to be created by Lizzie was *Twin Portrait* (1920), after the death of May.

6

Precipitated Portrait and Figure Painting

Although the Bangs sisters were well known for their art, there were two other spirit mediums who produced precipitated paintings, Allan B Campbell (1833-1919) and Charles Shourds (d.1926). Whilst both pairs of mediums lived at approximately the same time and worked in Lily Dale, there is no evidence that they ever worked together, even though their art is similar in its method of production. The art itself – and their personalities – were, however, very different from one another's.

English-born Campbell and American Shourds worked and met in Atlantic City, New Jersey, USA, as import-export merchants. Folk accounts suggest that they were 'boon companions', or same-sex partners. As mediums they worked within the spiritualist church movement alongside their independent work at Lily Dale Assembly.

Allan Campbell was first mentioned as having mediumistic powers in 1894 in the Pennsylvanian magazine *Cassadagan*, producing automatic and psychographic writing, and in 1896 it cites him as a spirit artist. Charles Shourds was leading materialisation séances each week and was only mentioned in 1897 as a medium working with Campbell. It was from this conjoining of mediumistic energies that the friends became good joint mediums; the fact that the Bangs sisters began working together a few years previously, and seemed successful, was perhaps why they joined forces.

The men's artwork was very different in style to their female counterparts'. Through their joint mediumship they created larger paintings in several art media, whereas the sisters produced generally the same sized paintings, pastelesque in media and also more emotive, less demonstrative in character.

Another difference between the two couples' work was that of the method by which they connected with the spirit world. As mentioned, the women knew they were mediums from childhood, whereas the mediumship of the two men had to weld together. They seem to have become masters of the development of mediumship in that they learned their trade through experimentation and finding out how to work with Spirit. There had to be a willingness to sit for many hours, attuning to invisible spirits and energies as well as accepting the manipulation of their own physical bodies. The Campbell 'brothers', in order to manifest this type of spirit art, would have done just that: create the appropriate conditions within which to work and then wait for spirit aides to manipulate and deposit earthly materials supporting the making of a picture.

Before they delivered a service they would say prayers and often those present would sing a hymn or song as though they believed that what they were doing was in service to God. (It is not known whether the Bangs sisters did the same although they would always begin a demonstration by explaining what they were going to do.) The brothers would set up a public séance carefully, describe what materials were to be used and how a spirit person would 'speak' through writing and by the image produced. They were very serious about their work, regarding it as spiritual. A proclamation was spoken at the beginning of each of their demonstrations:

"Ladies and Gentleman: you have come here for various purposes, and so I must explain before commencing demonstrations that we require of you and whosoever is not willing to submit to our rules please have your money returned to you and leave the place."

If anyone was there to protest or heckle then they were made to leave so that believers could enjoy the experience of such an unusual demonstration. Whilst this was an open meeting, nowadays meetings of materialisation or physical phenomena séances are completely closed to outsiders and held in locked rooms; the audience is usually there by invitation only. This is so that the participants can appreciate the full experience and, not least, for the safety of the medium.

With no formal art training, the partners first produced paintings supernaturally on porcelain, in a matter of a few minutes, by similar procedures as the Scottish artist David Duguid. Painting onto porcelain, especially of flowers, was a popular female pastime in America from the mid-nineteenth century. The supernatural art process appears to imitate this women's home craft movement. The style had been brought to New York by Staffordshire potters like Edward Lycett (1833-1910), as described by F Thistlethwaite in *The Atlantic Migration of Staffordshire Pottery Industry* (1958). Whilst actively encouraged by the Spiritualist Church in Atlantic City, the Campbell brothers' activities and salesmanship attracted non-spiritualists too because their work was like the craft that well-to-do women created during their afternoon gatherings.

Although merchants and salesmen, Allan and Charles also cleverly developed their talents as trance mediums and slate writers, specifically for their work as mediums and not as their only business. From New Jersey they moved to Lily Dale, taking a house together as life-long friends and partners. Elizabeth Harlow Goetz spoke at a memorial service for them after Charles died and her eulogy of him included mention of his philosophy in life: "Charles was a man who had no patience with deceit and hypocrisy and would denounce it whenever he discovered it…" The brothers treated each séance as a religious meeting and by remaining within the spiritualist environment, unlike the Bangs sisters, were in a better position to be defended against calls of trickery or financial gain. Even so, they were examined by investigators in the same way that the Bangs sisters were.

Belonging to, and working within, established churches and organisations gave them spiritual credence. By developing their mental mediumship through verbal messaging from the spirit world, together with producing automatic and trance art, Allan and Charles were also found by the church members they sat with in séance conditions to be physical mediums: they were able, like the Bangs sisters, to move objects with psychic energy alone. Working together, their supernatural energies became strong enough for the creation of psychographic spirit drawings on slates.

There is even one account of a spirit 'writing a letter' using a typewriter stored in the séance's cabinet (a fabric box in which the medium sat to build up psychic energy): "I am happy and have not found Heaven or Hell but am satisfied that I can come back and let my relatives know that I am still here." From the cabinet, a painting on cardboard of a lady then appeared and was given to a young man who accepted the writing, the portrait and the message.

The spiritualist magazine *Light of Truth* wrote in 1897 that the couple charged "…barely one tenth of that [the Bangs sisters'] price [$5.00] for their spirit art." Asking for so much less money at demonstrations and sittings gives the impression that they were more philanthropic than the Bangs sisters. Ron Nagy remarks that they "…held séances for people of average social background for the purpose of having a [deceased] loved one precipitate on the canvas." Perhaps in retaliation of the methods that the Bangs sisters employed, the brothers developed their own style of marketing their mediumship that concentrated on the spiritual aspect of the art rather than showmanship.

Although the couple worked in a very similar manner to the sisters, the processes they used in the production of their precipitated paintings were very different, facilitating large-scale paintings in oil on canvas in public. One folktale says that, after the death of Charles, oil paint was found on the ceiling above his bed as though he exuded paint while he slept… There is no explanation for this occurrence and the account cannot be verified since the Lily Dale house later burned down. (A spiritualist observation might be that he was psychically releasing himself of the excess paint not used in the production of precipitated oil paintings.)

The painting *Nora* (c.1898) represents one of the Campbells' pastelesque paintings produced around the turn of the twentieth century. This painting hangs in the Maplewood Hotel at Lily Dale and represents the spirit personality of a young girl. While studying this painting myself, I noticed that this image exhibits an aura of sadness, a sense of loss as though she, Nora, now mourns her own death. There is also a sense of loneliness in the image that gives the impression of the girl's grief at being absent from her living family. As a painting, *Nora* remains forever young, bringing to mind *The Picture of Dorian Grey* by Oscar Wilde; like the fictitious Grey, Nora is seen as a child clothed with the shroud of death, remaining young while others age.

A card placed next to this painting in the hotel reads:

"This lovely girls portrait was precipitated by the Campbell brothers around the turn of the century. By request of the deceased girls mother the portrait appeared in full light at an evening Campbell brothers auditorium séance. After the appearance of *Nora* on canvas the superstitious mother became alarmed because of her orthodox religious background and refused to accept this excellent work of precipitated art work calling it 'the work of the devil.' Thus the Assembly obtained one of the greatest works of art by the Campbell brothers." [sic]

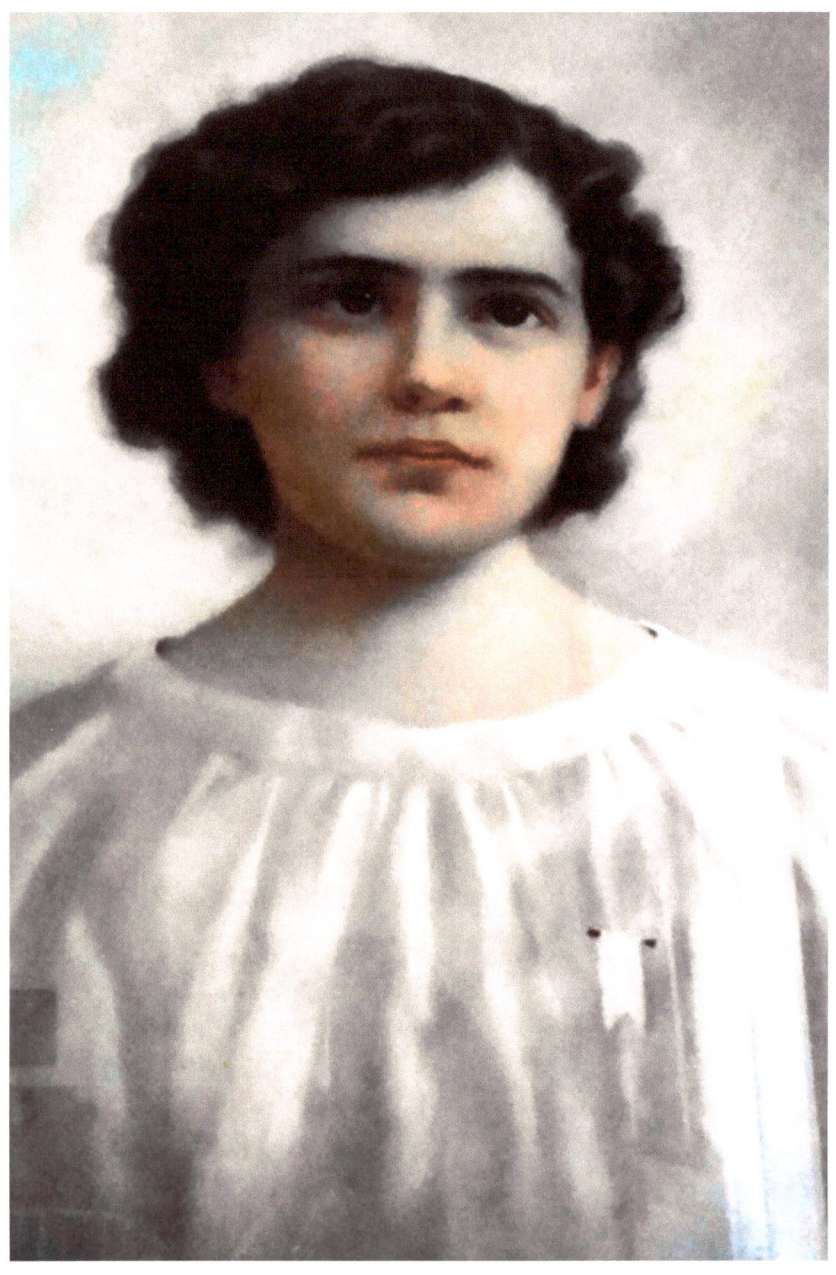

Nora

This portrait catches the eye. This may be either the aesthetic quality of the image or the sense of sadness that the image imparts. Nora floats in the centre of the picture in a mist of heavenly pinks and blues like an imaginary angel, her eyes tilted towards her new paradise.

However, the tag attached to the frame attests Christian, rather than spiritualist, concepts. 'This painting represents the divine presence of angelic life.' The notion of spiritual death, of Heaven and Hell, which the mother refers to, is not consistent with Spiritualism which holds that there is no Heaven or Hell in the spirit world but a continuous existence characterised by a person's acts upon the Earth. Nonetheless, both *Pearl* and *Nora* demonstrate, as well as the psychological sentiments of loss and grief, the continuation of the human soul.

Whilst the portrait of Nora was produced using similar supernatural methods to those of the Bangs sisters when creating *Pearl* and *Iola*, the brothers generated this painting at a public demonstration. Dust was reported to have been seen around the art surface and move about as it formed the image of the spirit. This would require the production of ectoplasm to create the movement and deposit of the dust. It would have been a mystical performance that astonished spectators, as they were asked to remove their hats in order to watch a cabinet being erected in which a painting was expected to emerge.

Yet completed in these open séance conditions is one of the most acclaimed of the Campbells' paintings, *Azur the Helper* (1898). This large and impressive oil painting, sized 40" x 60", was apparently the Campbells' spirit guide or helper. The painting is almost life-size, standing impressively head and shoulders above the viewer and almost dominating one wall in the lounge of the Maplewood Hotel, Lily Dale. It has been given pride of place to be viewed by spectators as they walk into the open lounge.

The painting was claimed to have been produced under strict séance conditions. The publication *Banner of Light*, on August 15th, 1898, stated that the painting, which was placed on a table against a large bay window, was produced in "one hour and thirty minutes" in front of six sitters who attested to its creation. The painting has been described as 'developing' on the canvas, giving the impression to some that photographic substances may have been used in the process, although this was never proven.

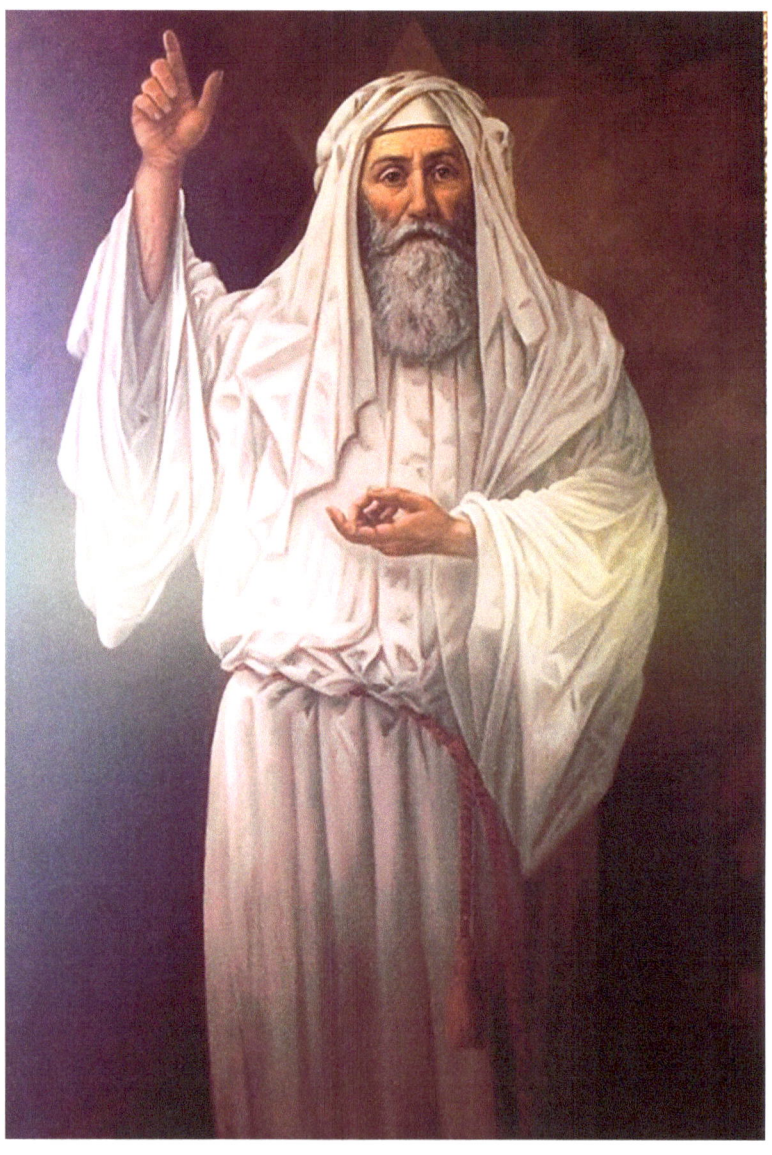

Azur the Helper

Since the painting is almost life-size, it is strangely overbearing. It was painted with oil-based paint on stretched canvas. Azur is dressed in a form of middle-eastern costume, perhaps indicating that this bearded figure is a holy man guiding the path of the Campbells in their spiritual work. The right hand points upwards towards God; the left hand has finger to thumb, a sign of the control of energies in Buddhist spirituality. Behind the head is a golden star with three points shown, perhaps indicating a Star of David.

Reading the painting symbolically, we seem to have a blend of religions here, the portrait representing the faiths of Islam, Judaism and Buddhism in one spiritual guide. There is no known description of this painting, leaving the spectator to make their own decision on this. Although spiritualists believe that they are guided by higher beings and that orthodox religion is irrelevant in the world of the Spirit, this painting seems to suggest that religion is of the Earth and not important to the spirit world.

The Campbells' images took the form of close portraits, head and shoulders of ordinary people, half-body portraiture with many details of dress and style and full life-size impressions of spirit guides and spiritual beings. Each image was created differently in style and colour with the eyes almost life-like.

Also hanging in the Maplewood Hotel is a precipitated painting of *Lincoln*. In the lapel of his jacket is a white flag. The addition of this flag is a characteristic of the precipitated artwork of the Campbells, perhaps a sign of the spirit artist. President Abraham Lincoln (1809-1865) was a man who invited mediums to his house for readings before the Civil War (1861-1865) and had few portraits painted in his lifetime; this spiritualist image, however, is highly representative of a photograph taken by Alexander Gardner in February, 1865, shortly before Lincoln was shot in April.

Comparing the photograph with the precipitated painting, it can clearly be seen that the two images are very similar, leading some to perpetuate the notion that a precipitated painting was produced using photographic techniques rather than by spirits. Yet there are also dissimilarities: the spirit portrait shows no mole; the chin is longer than the original, illustrated by the space between beard and lower lip; the hair is shown to be thicker and the skin healthier, with no blemishes. Perhaps the spirit world was indicating that there is no ill-health or disfigurement after death, all that ceasing with the physical body.

On the other hand, Ron Nagy suggests[45] that if the paintings are viewed with the use of iridology, the Campbells' painting "… reveals constitutional strengths and weaknesses, imbalances in the body, and your nutritional needs, as well as locating areas of toxic accumulation…" Alongside this interesting concept, that paintings of the eyes could indicate illnesses, Nagy also discusses a system by which the painting of Abraham Lincoln can be assessed in terms of 'facial diagnosis': that is, the reading of this portrait indicates certain health issues, now shown to be a correct analysis.

There is no doubt that the Bangs sisters' and the Campbell brothers' precipitated paintings are definitely interesting images independent of the landscape of Spiritualism and its idiosyncratic beliefs. The precipitated paintings seem more appealing to the eye than the experimental work of the English mediumistic automatists and trance artists, with their abstracted or Christian overtones. Mid-nineteenth century American spirit art is more appealing to the bereaved as portraiture that depicts the spirit beyond life.

These paintings were as mimetic of the spirituality inherent in the living as images of the deceased recreated in art. They have become models of the living self, appearing as enlightened impressions of the deceased. Holding an essence of the person's presence, spiritualists believing the portraits to be accurate representations of the deceased in their new lives as spirit entities.

All classifications of spirit art remain mysterious, however, and from these remarkable artworks there remains the conundrum of

---

[45] *Precipitated Spirit Paintings* (R. Nagy, Galde Press Inc, 2006)

how they could be produced so lifelike in such a short time. They were manifested as personal images for individuals unknown to the mediums, but now they remain as spiritualist relics of times past since precipitated paintings were never produced after 1920. The original artefacts are still exhibited in spiritualist museums and churches and yet, beyond the walls of Spiritualism, the general public has little awareness of the artefacts or their significance.

The question has to be asked: does belief in the supernatural mesmerise the séance sitter into thinking that the once happy spirit of a person has been captured in the portrait? The painting of Pearl, silent and muted now in her repose and appearing reclusive to the viewer, does not appear to demonstrate her innermost spirit, which spiritualists maintain exists after death.

Precipitated paintings have the appearance of traditional American folk art and psychographic art that of tattoo drawings. They are both forms of spirit art that are worked onto canvas or board and are representative of someone or something within the emotive sentimentality of spiritualist philosophy rather than of the bereaved.

But that is where similarity with art-as-object appears to end. A shift in thinking is required when considering art motivated by mediumistic physical phenomena philosophy, since the processes required to make psychographic drawing or precipitated painting did not follow the normal nineteenth or twentieth century rules pertaining to art in general. These works of spirit art, apparently, were not created by living artists but were believed to have been created solely by invisible, supernatural energies. This process is unique.

Whilst in modern times it is accepted that the energy of wind can create art, as in Yoko Ono's *Painting in the Wind* (1966), a problem still exists regarding the use of supernatural energies in the making of art. In Ono's concept of 'the invisible', the power of wind energy can be seen to be moving seeds out of holes in the fabric and where the seeds lie after the wind has gone is considered 'the painting' and can be recognisable to all. Yet paranormal energies may not be seen, felt or experienced by those in the precipitated séance conditions and so may not be believed. Supernatural energies are, in the main, typical to the experiencer but, unlike the wind, some may not believe in them.

It seems possible that if precipitated paintings were created now in the twenty-first century, when all forms of energy can be examined and an explanation approached, they may be better understood.

Early psychographic and precipitated art produced recognisable portraits of the deceased, supporting spiritualist principles, but their methods of production did not seem acceptable to non-spiritualists. So the work, although beautifully crafted, is hidden away in spiritualist camps, homes, museums and churches.

The next chapter examines the growth of spirit art as evidence of the continual existence of the human soul. It introduces the forerunners of 'evidential spirit art' and examines current artworks, whilst exploring contemporary methods of creating post-mortem portraits of the dead.

PART THREE

MENTAL MEDIUMSHIP

Modern Evidential Spirit Portraiture and Contemporary Spirit Art

FOREWORD

There was a time when people were happy to accept that what they believed a medium was producing was good and accurate. Perhaps a photograph could be used to offer 'proof' that the medium was producing what they said they were producing. There were sometimes drawings and paintings of 'guides' and other unrecognisable folk that were accepted and believed. However, there came a time when that was not what the public wanted and there was a shift in definition of what was acceptable as spirit art. Like the spirit messages given by a medium from the platform to a recipient, spirit art needed to have purpose and value – and, above all, be true.

Confirmation of the existence of life after death needed an earthly identity. Artists who were also mediums recognised that their art was an important part of spiritual belief because of its identifiable reality. Thus the photograph became both the tool for recognition of the deceased and validation of their presence in another world. The spirit portrait with a verifying photograph became the visual message, something that could be held, viewed and recognised. A spirit drawing or painting of a face – or of a familial object that belonged to the deceased, or of a landscape such as a house and its surroundings – were all impressions to suggest that life truly exists after death. Images or illustrations of where the deceased lived or worked were especially valuable. A pre-mortem photograph, when placed alongside a spirit art image, was difficult to deny as 'spiritual truth'. For the artist, it was also validation of their accurate mediumship and artistry.

Due to accusations of fraud against mediums and spirit artists during the nineteenth century, twentieth century spirit drawings required strong evidence to uphold public interest and engender spiritual belief. Family photographs had become readily available to the public through the opening of Kodak in Rochester, USA, in 1888. So by the twentieth century it had become ever more important for spirit portraits, of the deceased unknown to the artist, to be verified in this way as endorsement of the principle of the continuous existence of the human soul. Photographic substantiation seemed to offer solid proof.

A spirit portrait may define the deceased as though they were still living by features such as a turn of the head, a scar, an article of jewellery, the clothing or the hairstyle. These unique characteristics and affectations, together with other aspects of the drawing such as homely objects or a family animal, all provide information for the recognition of the deceased when placed alongside a photograph. These 'extras' gradually became the trademark of evidential and contemporary spirit art.

It is possible that the publication of Houdini's book, *A Magician Amongst the Spirits* [46], which attempted to discredit the earlier psychographic art as false, encouraged artists and mediums to develop a safer and less provocative style of art in their work. The photograph was evidence that spirit images were accurately illustrating the spirit world and that the artists could not be fraudulent. Thus there had to be a change in spiritualist practice. In particular, photographs would be supplied – by a stranger to the medium – *after* the event, easing suggestions that it could have been copied or that the medium had colluded with recipients of the portraits.

Whilst this part of the book begins with a discussion regarding the methods by which twentieth century evidential art was made, it is not my place to argue for or against the survival of the spirit. The paintings and drawings referred to, together with pre-mortem photographs, tell their own story.

---

[46] *A Magician Amongst the Spirits* (H Houdini, born Erik Weisz, Harper & Brothers, 1924; reprinted by Cambridge University Press, New York, 2011)

We shall consider the biographies and work of the most influential twentieth century artists who created spirit art as evidence of life beyond death. The first among this classification were Frank Leah (1886-1972) and Coral Polge (1924-2001), who were both mediums and artists. Whilst there have been several other spirit artists who created evidential art between 1930 and the present day, such as Ivor James (1922-1998), few have had as much acclaim as these two pioneers.

Since they died, subsequent spirit artists have followed the practice of collecting pre-mortem photographs to evidence their spirit-drawings after the production of their drawings. Frank and Coral defined the concepts and processes through which evidential spirit art was created and so should be considered the major artists for this classification.

Many of their drawings were treasured and framed, but others, especially when not clearly recognised, have been hidden away and never thought of again. It is unfortunate that this form of art did not have the ethos of a collectable piece of conventional artwork created by a famous artist. The worth or value of the piece is generally only felt by the person who recognises the deceased person in the drawing; the value and importance is in the emotion of the people who receive the portrait. It is noticeable that few spirit artists who began working in spiritualist churches and on community hall platforms since the 1930s have become key figures in art history. Whilst fame seems not to have mattered to them, that their portraits were recognised as accurate appears to be the only accolade they required. Recognition of their drawings mattered more than notoriety.

The two key figures, Frank Leah and Coral Polge, gave the latter part of their lives to working within the philosophy, beliefs and principles of Spiritualism, drawing with integrity that which they believed to be portraits of the dead or of spirit personalities[47].

---

[47] See especially *Living Images: The Story of a Psychic Artist* (C Polge and K Hunter, HarperCollins Publishers, 1991; reprinted by Regency Press, 1997)

Thus the following two chapters give a more detailed account of their life and work and includes accounts of how their art was created, the supernatural techniques used during the production of portraits and of the art methods and materials.

This period may perhaps be characterised as 'evidence before pictorial excellence'. The following chapter, however, will bring spirit art up to date as something that is not simply a tool for evidence of life beyond death. Spirit art is becoming an art form in its own right and has caught the eye of working and exhibiting artists, perhaps coming full circle to those pioneers who spent their lives attempting to bring their inspired images to the eyes of the public and the critics.

7

Mid-Twentieth Century Evidential Portrait Drawing

By experiencing clairvoyance in combination with an ability to draw, Frank Leah was able to recreate invisible spirits accurately. Maurice Barbanell, editor of *Psychic News,* described him as "…an artist for whom the dead pose in his studio", suggesting that the likenesses were so close in resemblance to the living person that it was as if the spirit were a model sitting beside him.[48] Alongside giving private readings in his studio flat in London, Frank demonstrated these creative techniques to audiences, including future spirit artists, in public halls and spiritualist churches. Photographs were brought by the recipients and given to him once a drawing had been made, or the recipient would send copies later to verify the portrait. This became a standard procedure that inspired future artists such as Coral Polge (and myself).

---

[48] *This is Spiritualism* (M Barbanell, Herbert Jenkins, 1959; reprinted by Spiritual Truth Press, 2001)

Paul Miller helps us to understand how Frank, as a mediumistic artist, created his spirit drawings.[49] Before the sitter arrived in his studio, Frank would 'see' the spirit person by clairvoyance and would then draw what he experienced. He also supernaturally gathered personal information regarding the deceased, without knowing the sitter or the deceased, and passed on this information to the recipient during the process of completing the portrait. His evidence was mostly very accurate and he had the ability to create a drawing without knowing the recipient at all. Miller states that, "…he sees with the eye of Spirit in a special way."

An artist in his own right and with great experience, Leah could draw portraits easily and, often in his own time without the recipient present, he would draw from what he could see in his mind's eye. This is clairvoyance: it is not an artist drawing from their imagination or conjuring up something in their mind that later appears to be the face of someone they have met before. It was said of Georgiana Houghton that she saw faces projected onto the paper she was looking at, in other words scrying for a face that she could copy. This method again is very different from clairvoyantly seeing faces, familial objects or landscapes directly related to the deceased. How would Leah know where the person lived or worked, what clothes they wore, how they managed their hair and so on before drawing them? He normally didn't know his client prior to their visit and indeed often produced the drawing prior to their arrival.

Leah did not lecture or teach the working practices of spirit art so it can be inferred that Coral Polge evolved her craft by observing him and then practising his techniques. In her own book, Coral described how she saw him working at public demonstrations and wished to work like him; from these experiences she began to create evidential spirit art in the same manner, by drawing what

---

[49] *Faces of the Living Dead: The Amazing Psychic Art of Frank Leah* (P Miller, Psychic Press, 1943; reprinted by Saturday Night Press Publications, 2010)

she referred to as "living images" of the dead. In turn, during my own training it was Coral's public demonstrations and private readings that inspired me to create spirit portraiture, replicating her methods.

To illustrate this point, I drew a portrait at a public demonstration of spirit art in Darmstadt, Germany, in 2008, and used the same method of working as Coral had learned from Frank, giving verbal evidence of name, age and illness before completing the portrait. The information was dictated to the audience through an interpreter and was given to a young German woman in the audience. I said the drawing was of her grandfather; however, she said that she did not recognise the person in the portrait at that time, although she did not know her Austrian grandfather.

Several months later the same woman emailed a digital copy of the portrait to her mother and it was confirmed that the image was a likeness of her deceased Austrian grandfather's passport photograph. Copies of the portrait and passport photograph were then emailed to me. The two images were very similar, offering confirmation that the grandfather's spirit was communicating to the recipient.[50]

Now, I do not speak German, nor the recipient English; we spoke through an interpreter so there was little scope for collusion. In the same manner, Coral Polge and Frank Leah would not know the recipients of their work and also had the ability to create recognisable portraits without understanding the language of the person – even without meeting the person at all.

To contrast their methods, Coral would make a clairsentient connection with a discarnate consciousness and begin to draw what she felt, due to the impulse of a spirit guide – she believed that the guide would draw the spirit through her. She drew in pastel on Ingres paper, taking approximately ten to fifteen minutes. Frank worked from his studio or visited people's homes,

---

[50] *Portraits from Spirit* (A Bridge Davies, AuthorHouse UK, 2011)

where he would draw his portraits in about ten seconds, using his trained art abilities. He is reported to have said that during the connection and replication of drawing close to the spirit world, "I died a thousand deaths [and] frequently took on, in painful replication, the last physical experiences of those spirits who presented themselves to be portrayed."

Maurice Barbanell wrote, "Leah is definitely unusual. He lives in a world of his own, has the artistic temperament, which makes him become heated over matters that others might dismiss, and possesses a volubility that has to be heard to be appreciated. He has been clairvoyant since he was a child. At first, he was scared of the forms he could see but which were invisible to others. He was mystified as to who these forms were, until gradually it dawned on him that they belonged to those the world calls dead. For many years, he followed the normal vocations of being a journalist and a cartoonist until, one day, he decided to combine all his gifts."[51]

Frank Leah did not come to this form of working with the spirits of the dead lightly. Originally, his work involved drawing cartoons of the actors, writers and wealthy people of Dublin's fair city during the 1920s. He was a celebrated newspaper figure in Dublin, also well known as an artist, draughtsman, sculptor and journalist.

His life began humbly as one of nine children in Stockport, England, towards the end of the industrial revolution years. By the age of twelve he had demonstrated a gift for drawing by selling one of his artworks and three years later he attended the Glasgow School of Art. Then at nineteen he began training as a journalist in Dublin, here becoming Art Editor to five city-based newspapers, including the *Weekly Freeman*, gaining a reputation for creating mostly 'lightning' cartoons of the Dublin elite and thespians of the Abbey Theatre.

It was through these groups that he met people who helped him in his artistic work, such as the Irish Literary Revival set and the playwrights and artists W B Yates, Lady Gregory, Sean

---

[51] *Power of the Spirit* (M Barbanell, Spiritualist Press, 1949)

O'Casey and John Millington Synge. These people were pleased that he would turn up at events with his paper and pencil or pen and ink. Irish archivist and historian, Harriett Wheelock, in *Gleanings on Sir Charles Cameron* (1830-1921, Dublin's Chief Medical Officer) notes that, "Finally, there is a sketch made of Cameron by the artist Frank Leah. This drawing was made just one week before Cameron's death on the 27th February, 1921."

Thus Frank Leah made his name as an artist and many of his artworks from this era are now carefully collated in the Hathaway Collection in Dublin's City Library. I was fortunate enough to be invited by the curator, in 2014, to view the Collection where I had the pleasure of seeing about one hundred and fifty examples of Frank's sketches; they were mostly of those individuals above, but there were none of his spiritual character drawings. (These caricatured portraits are so precious that I was only the second person to view them.) This is a unique selection of Frank's non-spiritual work, and it indicates that his life between 1918 and the mid-1920s did not have any relationship to the spiritualist movement.

While in Ireland, Frank drew images of the famous people around him and it is clear that he was praised and sought-after in Dublin. So why did he leave such a creatively invigorating place in which to live?

He is not referred to at all as a spirit artist during his life there and his spirit artwork only appeared when he relocated to London; even so, information about him at that time is quite vague. Ireland was in a state of political chaos towards the end of the 1920s and many of the actors and writers with whom Frank had become friendly were leaving for America and Britain. His interest in spirit drawing must have grown later, when he moved from Ireland to work in London's Fleet Street, the home of British journalism.

The journal *Irish Comics* states that, after he moved to London, he "…became a psychic-artist, painting the 'spirits' he perceived accompanying his sitters." There is no mention in the London papers about him until he began to produce spirit portraiture.

Then, about a decade after moving to England, he was mentioned in *The Journal of the Society for Psychical Research*, 1939, as among a number of mediums who were to be examined by the Research Department of the Society (the SPR, London). Here it was reported that his spirit portraiture was to be examined as one of thirteen 'spontaneous' cases of mediumship chosen for investigation by the SPR for his artistic mediumship. The journal stated that, "Among other mediums examined is Mr Frank Leah, the artist, who makes sketches of alleged communicators. Several sittings have been arranged by the Society, the notes of which may be seen on demand." However, there is no evidence of Frank's examination and in the same SPR journal it was reported that only four mediums were "worth studying". Perhaps Frank Leah was not one of them!

As a spirit artist, Leah claimed to draw guided by the sensations he received from what he believed was the spirit world. This was in quite a different manner to that of his earlier caricatures, yet what he was very good at was recreating a 'visual signature' of the deceased spirit. His spirit drawings, when compared with the corresponding photographs supplied by their recipients, are surprisingly similar in profile, dress, hair and adornments. These familial objects were the evidence that Spiritualism was looking for in order to provide proof of life beyond death. The drawings are always life-size and were done in daylight. Paul Miller's biography contains photographs accompanying drawings, as evidence of his ability to create images that genuinely looked like their deceased subjects.

Miller maintains that Frank created spirit portraits both when 'inspired' and 'on demand' from the spirit world; and, like the drawings he had produced in Ireland, they were strong, determined pencil sketches. With the accuracy of his work, he set a high standard for other spirit artists to follow. Remember, though, that these were drawings of and for people he had never met and had no prior knowledge of. He "…received sitters, all anonymously, through spiritualist societies… [and] many of the drawings are made in his mind – if not, in fact, on paper – before the sitters arrive." He claimed to draw from the *sensations* he received from what he believed was the spirit world and would remark that the spirits of the dead were "vibrantly alive" and not dead.

"Leah maintains," Barbanell continued, "that there is nothing ghostly or eerie about these spirit visitors. He does not see them as phantoms, wraiths or transparent figures. They look solid. They are alive and intensely vital. He can walk round them as though they were living persons on Earth, just as if they were models posing for an artist. They will stand still while he takes a note of their shape, proportions and any other identifiable details. When they are experienced communicators, they show themselves very clearly… every line and wrinkle, the colour of the eyes and hair, and even… individual characteristics, such as a mole or a broken tooth. Usually, they give the kind of information about themselves that produces speedy recognition, unusual names, the towns in which they lived and their professions. He is not in trance when he executes these drawings. He is quite normal."

Leah drew very quickly, according to his patrons with lightning speed. (Possibly this was because mediumship was still illegal at that time and so was practised covertly.[52]) On one occasion he drew seven portraits, aged from boy to man, within a minute or so. Now, in the twenty-first century we recognise this as an indication that he drew automatically as well as clairvoyantly. He also drew in the dark or at dusk, and if visiting others would ask for the lights to be turned down.

Many of his clients were not very well off and he found it difficult to ask payment for a portrait, although he did ask for travel

---

[52] In the UK, drawing spirit portraits came under the Witchcraft Act, 1735, which was only repealed in 1951. It was replaced by the Fraudulent Mediums Act, to safeguard vulnerable people against illicit psychics, and this was in turn repealed in 2008.

money. Given that he was truly gifted and somewhat famous from his work in Ireland, this is remarkable. On the other hand, sometimes his subjects in the spirit world would ask for the money on his behalf during their readings… This seems a little strange, but perhaps those in the spirit world knew how much the clients had in their pockets!

As well as working clairvoyantly and automatically in his own right, when Frank Leah attended others' transfiguration or physical séances he would see spirit faces overshadow the face of the medium. With his previous experience of the theatre and with famous actors in Dublin, he once took the opportunity to sit in a séance alongside London's Drury Lane actors and theatre-goers. In the dark, he could see clairvoyantly the actor Cowley Wright in costume, which he drew. The story is told by Paul Miller in his biography of Leah.

"This drawing was done in the dark while [Harold] Shape was entranced, and as Leah finished his work he asked [Cowley Wright], 'Is that right?' The [spirit] guide answered, 'It is perfect, except for the mouth. You have mistaken my medium's mouth, with the false teeth, for mine. I will try to show myself more clearly.' The medium was then transfigured and in the dark altered the mouth, the guide remarking at the end that it matched his own mouth better and made him look older than the medium…"

Only in rare circumstances did Leah draw the portraits of those in the spirit world known as guides. This experience helped him to understand that he was also able to draw the portraits of those in the spirit world who attempt to help us here, as well as his other work.

Gwen Byrne, the owner of one of Frank's portraits, speaks from personal experience in her book *Russell*, an emotional story about her deceased son.[53] She describes Frank as "a small grey-haired man, rather bent over… a bit grouchy, but kind." Frank had produced for her – in her absence, because she was late for

---

[53] *Russell* (G Byrne, Janus Publishing Company, 1994)

the appointment – a portrait of Russell without prior knowledge of either of them other than an earlier telephone call.

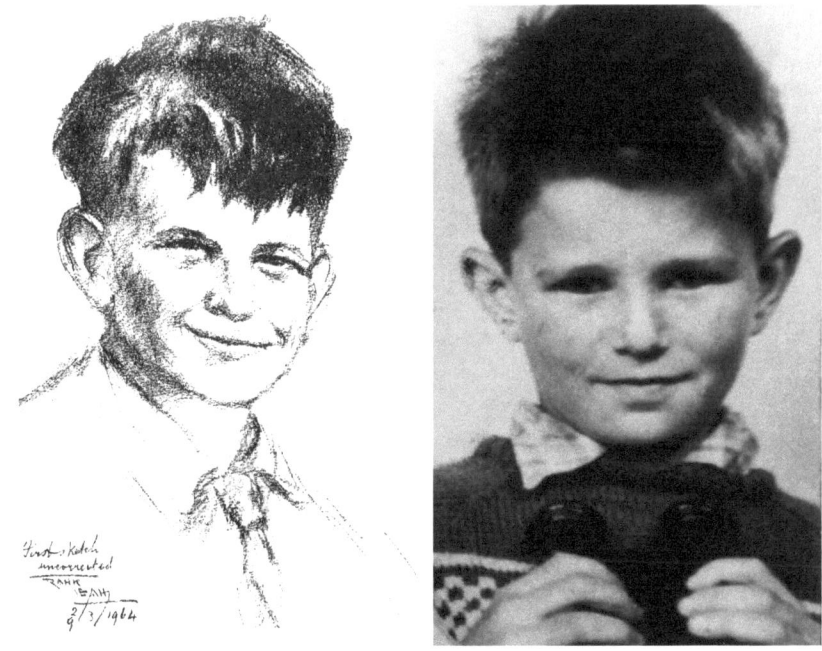

Russell   *Photograph of Russell*

He did this many times and Miller mentions it in a chapter concerning one Shirley Ann Woods, a six year-old child who had died from an incurable disease.

"Mrs Woods was a Roman Catholic… and the law of Rome is that Spiritualism… is outlawed… Mrs Woods pursued her quest [to find the truth after her daughter's death]. She telephoned Leah at 11 p.m. The artist was not told what was wanted, but he informed Mrs Woods that she wanted a portrait of her child. And he described [the daughter] exactly, remarking on her 'dark, dank hair', describing her eyes, her slight figure, pale complexion and penetrating look, and he then outlined her character."

In general, Frank's spirit portraits were certainly fair likenesses of the deceased; indeed, an artist drawing from life may not be able to demonstrate as good a likeness of his subject unless drawing from a photograph. Yet this was not the case with Frank's drawing for Mrs Woods, according to Miller's biography. In this, he drew the parting in the girl's hair and the slight gap where the fringe and parting meet, exactly as the girl's parents later confirmed – without having met the girl or either parent. Mrs Woods described the portrait as "a splendid likeness".[54] But there was more to come... Mrs Woods' husband later called at Leah's studio, and was impressed by the portrait. In his presence, Leah did a second portrait with added details of the daughter's appearance. In both drawings the child was shown wearing a distinctive plaid frock, which her parents recognised because they had kept it.

The astonishing sequel to the story is that, not long afterwards, Mrs Woods had a sitting with the medium Estelle Roberts, through whom the child referred to the portraits that Frank Leah had done. The mother had not mentioned this fact to Estelle. The accuracy of the drawings and subsequent message is taken by spiritualists to be proof that the spirit of the girl is still alive, albeit in another world.

Portrait of a Man (1938) is one of the few spirit works Leah created that show familial objects in the drawing. The Irish gentleman, otherwise now unknown, is shown with his pipe. Frank Leah was the first of the spirit artists to demonstrate genuinely evidential spirit portraiture as proof for life existing beyond death. We do not know whether it was his idea, but he was the first spirit artist regularly to use a photograph owned by the recipient of a drawing as a means of identifying the portrait. For spiritualists and others, this was strong supportive evidence for the principle of the continuous existence of the human soul, these drawings simply showing that a human being or animal has survived death. There is no evidence that any of his drawings were replicas of the deceased, since he had never met them.

---

[54] The parents produced a photograph as evidence, which is reproduced in *Faces of the Living Dead* (cf. reference 49).

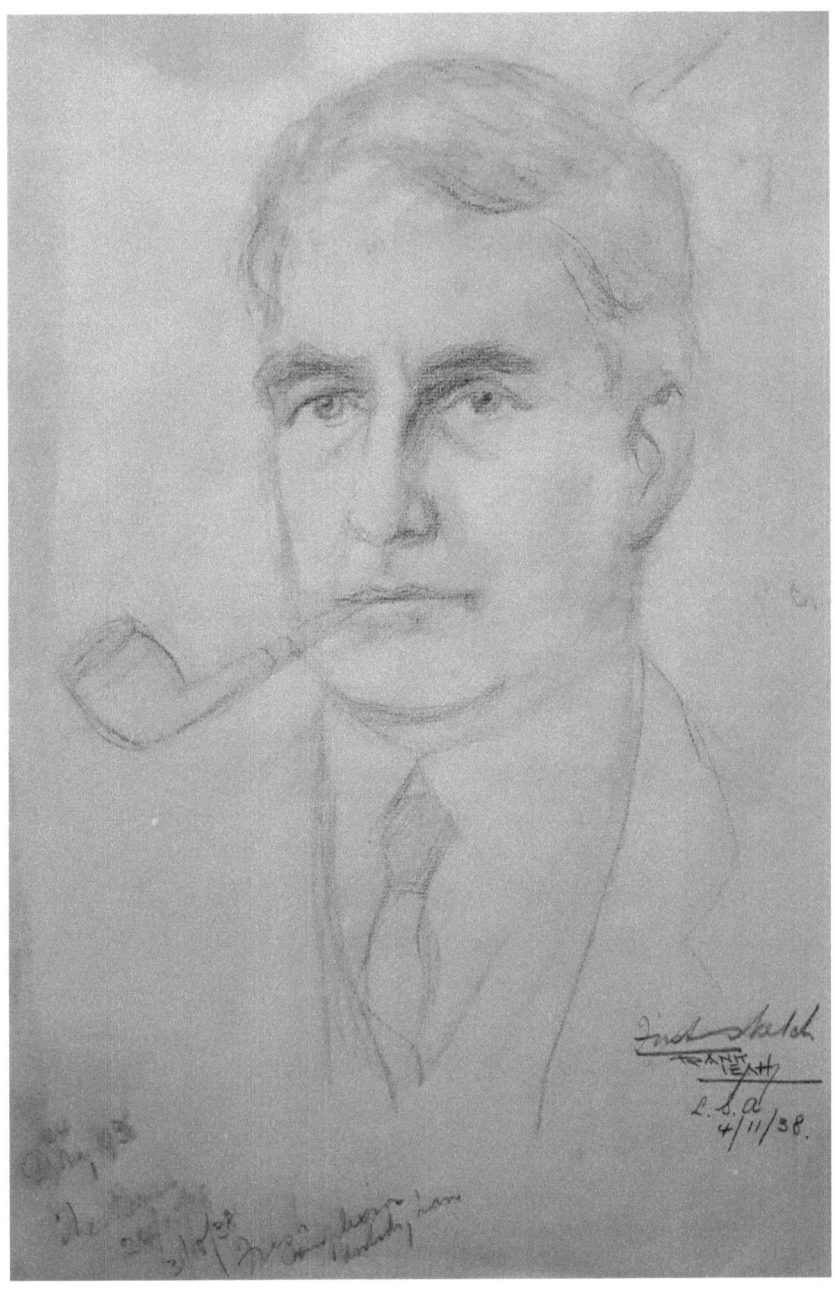

Portrait of a Man

"When critics jeer at fortune-telling and confuse it with Spiritualism," writes Paul Miller, "and when they talk about back-parlour séances as though we were still in the Victorian era… they forget or ignore the vast body of factual knowledge that has been built up."

The photographs provided after the drawing had been made were the factual knowledge illustrating that an artist, with the inherent skill of mediumship, is not a fortune-teller but someone who can illustrate another world beyond the physical.

"For thirty years…" wrote Maurice Barbanell, "Leah has used his combined talents of clairvoyance and artistry to portray thousands of dead women and children. In nearly every case, because these drawings have been identified by relatives or friends of the subjects, they provide permanent proofs of survival. He has died thousands of deaths, for inevitably he has to reproduce on himself the final earthly conditions of the people who came to life on his easel."

He was able and willing to create what he was convinced were truthful portrait impressions of the spirits of the deceased, thus encouraging evidential and contemporary spirit art to be produced in this way providing evidence of an afterlife. His drawing of the spirit of Russell, for example, shows that he was able to draw a portrait of the deceased without having met the child and even without the mother being present.

In later years, Frank Leah lived a somewhat lonely and simple life, yet he left the world an extraordinary legacy in the form of drawings of the spirits of the deceased, who kept appearing before him. He was an inspiration to others, such as Coral Polge, and was acknowledged by prominent spiritualists such as Harry Boddington as providing powerful evidence in defence of the life-after-death principle.

In my opinion, it is important that today's spirit artists go through the same gradual developmental processes as Leah, as though one is being trained to make recognisable visual representations of the once living. Whether the medium has a natural talent for art or not, this is a slow process but vital in making the work more evidential. Frank Leah had already done twenty years of apprenticeship in Dublin as a caricaturist. This gave him an invaluable backdrop to his future work as a spirit artist, being able to draw what he saw, felt or sensed. He was the forerunner of spirit art in contemporary times.

8
Late Twentieth Century Evidential Drawing

We can say that this classification of evidential spirit art originated with Frank Leah in the early 1930s, followed by Coral Polge in the early 1970s. Both Frank and Coral were trained artists and so the methods by which they drew their spirit portraits were due to their training as well as their experience as mediums. With their ability to draw well, together with their knowledge and belief in the supernatural, they sketched, drew and painted easily identifiable portraits.

These two major artists are now deceased, so my information about Coral is from personal meetings with her, from her autobiography and from people who had private readings with her. There are also written records and books about, or written by, her alongside case study information.

By examination of both Coral Polge's and Frank Leah's methods of working there is clear evidence that their demonstrations and teachings transformed spirit art. Between the turn of the twentieth century and about 1930, the content and working methods of spirit art changed so that any claims of fraud could be challenged and it is clear that both Frank and then Coral designed their methods so that their portraits could be validated.

In her autobiography, Coral Polge writes of Frank Leah's influence on her work and she in turn carried his working methods forward to future spirit artists. Her public presentations and teachings certainly influenced Ivor James and contemporary artist Alan Stuttle (and myself, during the early stages of my development). Their demonstrations and private readings established a movement of spirit art through their lineage that emerged from their experimentation with supernatural techniques and artistic processes. Thus Leah's and Polge's indirect guidance influenced an entire art movement into the twenty-first century, albeit one that has hardly been recognised by the art world.

Exploring these artists alongside other contemporary living spirit artists, we find that each artist develops his or her own style when producing impressions of the spirits of the dead. We have already noted some differences between Coral's art and that of Frank. Most such artists will tune in to what they believe to be a spirit consciousness and then create a drawing or painting from the supernatural impressions they perceive. Contemporary artist Alan Stuttle suggests this very point in his own book, *The Psychic Artist*.[55]

When an image is recognised by a recipient, this provides credibility for the artist and for the conviction that the spirits of the deceased can survive death and communicate with us. From my own observations of public demonstrations, I have found that typically five or six images are drawn by the artist with perhaps only two or three of them positively recognised at the time. On the other hand, it must be said that it has often been the case that once the recipient has returned home and checked the portrait, for example, against a photograph that may have been taken many

---

[55] *The Psychic Artist – Are You Ready for the Challenge?* (A Stuttle, ed. J Elliot, self-published, 2007)

years before the recipient was born, there may then be positive recognition. This, of course, offers even stronger evidence and a stronger defence against any suggestion of collusion. Leah and Polge instigated changes in the creation of spirit art so that images contained more evidence of survival.

Whilst artistic skills are very important when producing the portraits, supernatural abilities are necessary too. Coral Polge admits in her autobiography that, in the early stages of her mediumship, few of her drawings were recognised. Yet she knew that recognition was a vital ingredient of the evidential process. Sensitively, she proposed that her "artist's eye was not fully developed" and that she required more practice when drawing spirit portraits. In the beginning she spent many years honing her craft so that her drawings and pastel paintings would become more recognisable.

Spirit portraiture, though, is a two-edged sword. As well as the drawings appearing good, a medium requires the development of their psychic skills: the art and the mediumship are symbiotic. And although an ability to see, hear or sense the spirit world is necessary in order to create spirit portraits, not all spirit artists were, or are, mediums as such. A person can learn to create recognisable portraits through watching a spirit artist at work or by attending classes. Understanding can especially be gained by working alongside an experienced medium producing portraits with another person giving a message.

This is one of the processes that Coral Polge went through as she worked with Gordon Higginson (1918-1993), an eminent medium and President of the Spiritualists' National Union. In 1985, I met and witnessed Coral working with Gordon at the Arthur Findlay College, Stansted Hall. At that meeting, I received a drawing on acetate of a lady called Mary whom I had met only once; Gordon gave me information about this lady while Coral drew a simple and linear portrait in black ink. I did recognise the lady although I was rather surprised to receive both verbal and visual messages from a deceased person whom I had not known well.

Coral Polge was the first spirit artist to create portraits on acetate with black marker pen, enabling future spirit artists to work 'outside the box' of only using pastels or pencils when drawing. She created *Grandmother* (c.1990) for a friend of mine, who wrote the following accompanying comment:

"The picture is of my grandmother who died before I was born, but she does resemble family photographs. This was drawn at a demonstration of psychic art in the library at Stansted Hall."

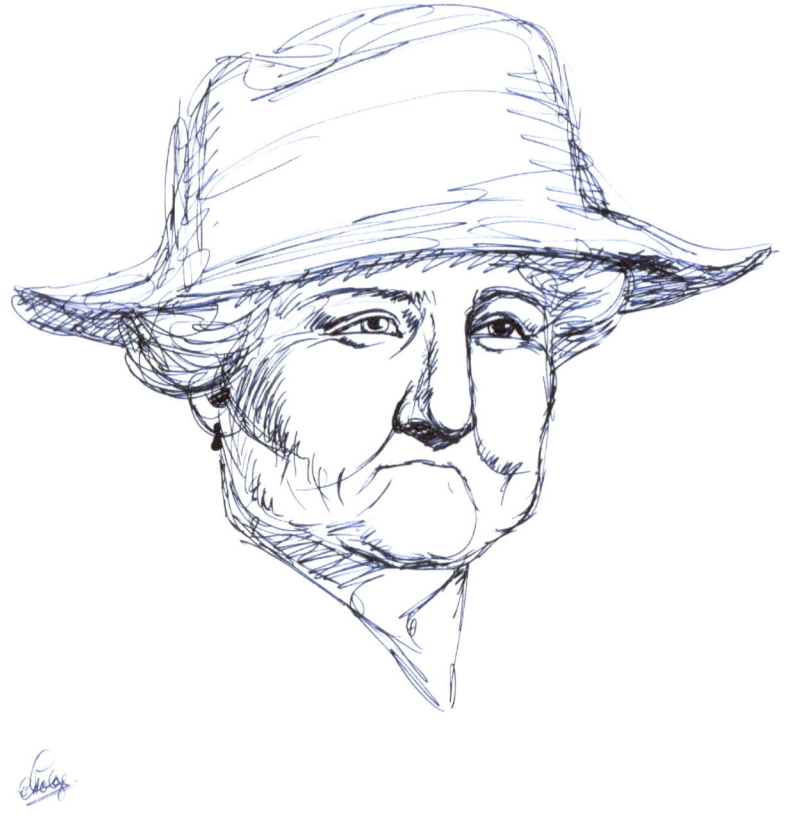

Grandmother

Gordon Higginson is claimed by many to have been the greatest spiritualist medium in the world. He was born and died in Stoke on Trent, England, and was taught mediumship from childhood by his mother Florence (Fanny) Higginson. When working with Coral Polge on a public stage, he would make the link with a spirit presence while Coral drew the portrait, sometimes in pastels and occasionally on acetate sheet with an overhead projector. Thus their combined mediumship generated both a drawing and a verbal message for a recipient. In the 1980s, churches and halls were always full for their demonstrations, sometimes with people standing outside, because a medium working with an artist was always considered very accurate and sought after.

As a trained graphic artist, like Frank Leah, she had the ability to draw what she considered to be spirit people without having known them. She said that she was clairsentient and could feel the personality of the spirit when she was drawing, as well as having an ability to hear descriptions of the spirit clairaudiently. These are two major supernatural abilities that aided her practice.

However, she found it difficult to develop her mediumship, stating that she struggled at first to find the right circle of people to sit with in the manner of a séance. The practice of 'sitting' for the development of mediumship is a relic of the Victorian era and, even today, potential mediums begin to draw the spirit world by sitting with other novices in home circles or at spiritualist church classes. In this way the novice is able to cultivate what is considered to be a natural gift that can be developed through being taught by an experienced medium.

From her development as a medium, Coral became a lecturer at the Arthur Findlay College in Stansted and at the College of Psychic Studies in London. There she began to influence future spirit artists, including the working artist and Royal College of Art watercolourist, Alan Stuttle. Through her teaching and demonstrations in the public arena around the world, she established her own creative production methods. Once she had gained confidence in her own work, she began to influence a second wave of evidential contemporary spirit artists. The manner in which Coral demonstrated her work publicly was partly as a result of Frank's influence. By demonstrating to the general public what they termed 'psychic art' (referred to as 'spirit art' after 1990), Frank Leah and Coral Polge were the first in the twentieth century of the major contributors to the advancement of this classification of art that offered hard evidence.

Unlike the previous Victorian female pioneer, Georgiana Houghton, the first evidential spirit artists did not formally exhibit their paintings and drawings, as would conventional artists. There is no evidence that Leah exhibited spirit art in his lifetime, whilst Polge is reported only to have exhibited her work before a demonstration of Spiritualist Art at Claxton Hall.[56] However, they did and still do ask payment for their works, which had been frowned upon in the Victorian era because payment for a spiritual activity was deemed unacceptable. Both Frank and Coral did charge for their work.

Coral referred to this "awkward issue" in her book stating that, "…my parting from Arthur [her husband] meant that I was faced with having to earn a living from my work." These artists were paid for private sittings at spiritualist churches and at the Arthur Findlay College, as spirit mediums are today. It is noteworthy that whilst many contemporary spirit artists could earn money from their work, most of them still give their work free to the recipients of their portraits.

Coral Polge thought of Frank Leah as a mentor, describing the demonstrations of accurate spirit portraiture that she saw him creating and saying, "The greatest psychic artist of the time, Frank Leah, whom I felt I could never emulate, gave one public demonstration

---

[56] Such art has now been exhibited on three occasions at the Ancient High House in Stafford, England, between 2007 and 2010 under the name of the Spirit Art Society.

in 1957, which I attended. His demonstration was unusual in that he had made his preliminary contacts with recipients by telephone, gaining impressions simply from the voice, and making quick sketches. He took these pictures to the hall where the demonstration was held, and finished off the portraits on the platform."

Although she showed clear admiration for his work, she felt that she was not able to create her portraits in the same manner, which is what she had hoped to do. At first, she produced similar drawings by using only a pencil. Then, after his death in 1972 and when she became more popular, being invited to other countries such as Australia, Italy and Germany to demonstrate, she began to experiment with pastels.

A few of her portraits were exhibited before a performance in Caxton Hall, London, and they "evoked a lot of interest"; yet, unfortunately, few drawings were accepted as being evidential, as true likenesses. She openly admits this in her autobiography. But as she practised, her pastel portraits became more evidential and recognised by their recipients. She now began drawing what she referred to as the "living images" of the dead. Once she realised that she was able to create portraits that people recognised as their loved ones, Coral had completed her development. She had come into her own as a spirit artist and her art became acknowledged and convincing both within the spiritualist arena and to the public.

The same friend whose *Grandmother* was shown earlier, says of the drawing *Spirit Guide*, "This picture is of someone close to me at the time I was sitting in a closed [development] circle. It was drawn in the Blue Room at Stansted Hall in 1988."

Coral Polge created many such drawings of spirit guides for those who had private sittings in spiritualist churches or at Stansted Hall, as well as more evidential works. She herself said that whilst people felt that they knew who had been drawn, they often had to go home and ask others for evidential recognition; this invariably came in the form of photographs. She did most of her work in the 1980s but many of her portraits have been lost over time.

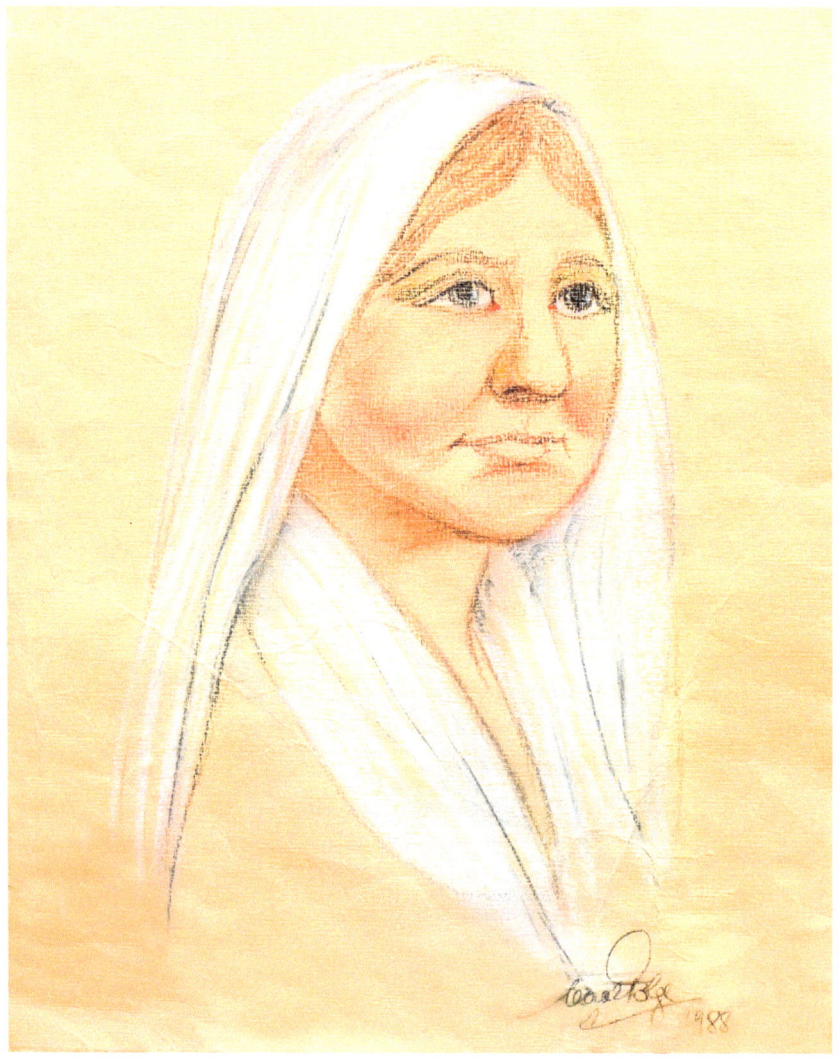

Spirit Guide

A correctly identified drawing supported by a photograph typifies the modern evidential classification. They are usually quickly produced portraits, combined with a few sentences of verbal information regarding the deceased during life, aimed to support the philosophy of Spiritualism. A further example is my own drawing of a young girl, Hollie (also see Chapter 9).

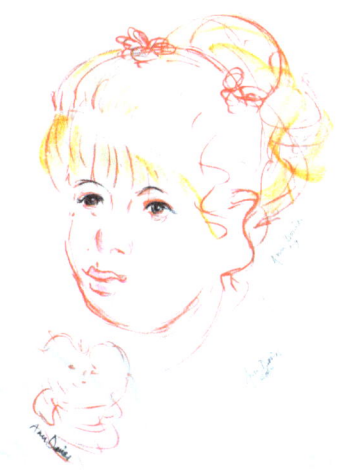 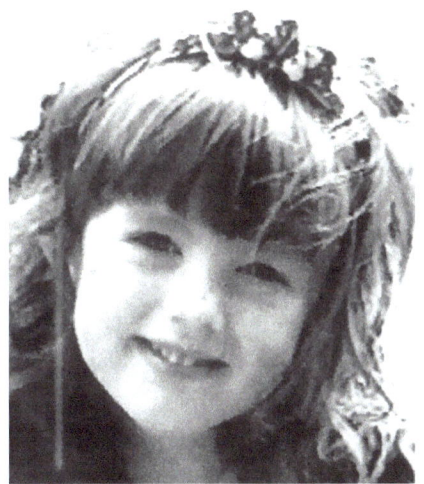

Hollie   *Photograph of Hollie*

A different philosophical issue, though, rather muddied the spiritual waters at times. Whilst Frank Leah knew that he drew spirit portraits by his own abilities, there was a growing fashion in spiritualist circles to engage with an 'artist-in-spirit' (often a renowned figure of history) who would create the drawings and paintings for them. Such a link cannot be proved. Furthermore, sought-after images of one's spirit guide could hardly ever be recognised by photographic evidence and so were not completely accepted by old-school spiritualists.

Coral Polge was herself aware of this paradox when she referred to some of her drawings as "cannot be identified". In order to ascertain who her own spirit guide was, and before she found an image of him, she drew a pencil portrait of the spirit she sensed with her as she drew. The result was a drawing later identified as the eighteenth century pastel artist Maurice de la Tour (1704-1788). She said she saw de la Tour as a spirit guide who overshadowed her while she worked.

As a symbiotic process, many spirit artists willingly allow themselves to be manipulated or possessed by what they believe to be their spirit guides. This was first experienced by John Murray

Spear, the Victorian automatists, Georgiana Houghton and the trance artist David Duguid. Polge believed this to be so because, like de la Tour, she produced artwork in pencil or pastel. This belief that a guide helps the artist was not a new idea, since the writer and historian Charles Colbert reports that the nineteenth century American luminist landscape painter George Inness (1825-1894) believed his paintings to be guided by the Venetian School's Tintoretto (1518-1594).[57]

Spirit mediums have the conviction that they are helped, or led, by one or more spirit guides. These may have been family members or complete strangers who appear willing to help them. Although support from people in the spirit world seems very helpful for the medium, a conundrum arises when we compare, say, images of Native American leaders and tribesmen, drawn from life for example by the artists Charles Bird King (1785-1862) and George Catlin (1796-1872), with Coral Polge's guide-influenced pictures. Whilst Coral was convinced that her work was influenced and drawn by a deceased accomplished artist, her drawings seem naïve in comparison with the work of these other artists. (This anomaly reappears in contemporary spirit art since some of our contemporary artists are convinced that they are influenced by the spirits of Frank Leah or Coral Polge.)

Coral's rendition appears glamorised beside the art of those nineteenth century artists. When we examine Catlin's version of a chief of the Blackfoot tribe painted from life, it differs greatly in artistic quality from the stylised drawing of a spirit guide by Coral. Indeed, few of the tribe leaders painted by Catlin could be compared to her romanticised impressions of Native American spirit guides. The archetype of such spirit guides is prevalent in spiritualist culture, especially in the form of Silver Birch and White Eagle who communicated through Maurice Barbanell.

---

[57] *Haunted Visions: Spiritualism and American Art* (C Colbert, University of Pennsylvania Press, 2011)

Since her beginnings in 1959, Coral Polge was an advocate for spirit art, spreading the techniques and knowledge worldwide. After her death in 2001 due to cancer, such work remained in a procedural void of worship in her memory until artists such as Alan Stuttle, Su Wood and Lyn Cottrell began to teach drawing and painting in the style of Frank Leah and Coral Polge. Thus the movement of spirit art as evidence for life after death continued.

Frank and Coral created evidential spirit art in their unique styles, their individual experiences as trained artists and mediums supporting their creativity, a process not much in evidence before 1930. While Spiritualism, as a series of principles of belief, remained the same, the artists became more creative by experimenting with different forms of supernaturalism. Their objective was not to introduce evidential spirit art as born-again psychic portraiture from the Victorian era, but to demonstrate that in the twentieth century the work could also be experimental and innovative.

These two pioneers were forebears of unusual supernatural creative techniques that developed after them and influenced the second and third wave of spirit artists. The next chapter describes a significant change in the phenomenon, though, as the twenty-first century arrived and, with it, the digital age. There are new artists, animators and photographers; many are working artists and mediums too in their own right. But instead of just following the lead of predecessors, the next stage of evidential spirit art has moved on, manifesting new forms of art that utilise more than pencil and paper or brush and canvas.

9
Contemporary Spirit Art

The supernatural procedures used in the creation of contemporary spirit art differ from previous classifications, including modern spirit art, especially regarding verification as evidence. In the mid-nineteenth century, the confirmation of spirit portraiture was a matter of faith alone for both the medium and the recipient, since evidence in the form of a photograph or a painted portrait was not as readily available as it is today. Towards the end of that century, photographic evidence in support of spirit drawings began to appear. This helped to promote the spiritualist faith – and belief in survival – as photography gave the art credibility. Spiritualist belief remained the same but the art began to change, with new and creative innovations evolving the movement.

Photographic images have become the key to identification of a deceased person in a spirit drawing, something that is now almost spontaneous as an artist completes an impression of the person in spirit. Those who attend public demonstrations often have photographic proof with them in their pockets, on mobile 'phones or other digital devices, so this is the first time in history that confirmation can be easy and immediate.

During modern demonstrations of spirit art, it is common practice that the person who recognises a drawing, and has proof of the deceased, receives the drawing. Illustrating this point, I created a drawing of a young girl in 2009 at a public demonstration at Walsall Spiritualist Church, in the West Midlands, England. The drawing was accepted by the child's grandmother, who had photographic evidence of the girl with her. Indeed, within seconds of the drawing being started and the child's name, Hollie, being spoken, the grandmother had taken out her mobile 'phone with a photograph of the child on it, which she then displayed to the audience. Naturally, I did not know the child or grandmother and had not seen the photograph before the demonstration. (The image is shown in Chapter Eight.)

This event caused quite a stir since many in the audience had known the little girl and had witnessed her as a bridesmaid at her mother's wedding. My spoken evidence of name, cause of death and "butterflies in her hair" was fully accepted too. There is often a sense of shock when recognition of the subject comes early in the creation of a portrait, as it was with the drawing of Hollie. Nowadays, if the portrait can be identified straight away this gives credence to the artist creating the work as a bona fide medium.

It should be admitted, though, that such use of a photograph as evidence in support of a spirit portrait has been questioned several times in the history of spirit art. Spiritualists would define the photograph, or whatever image leads to recognition of the portrait, as proof that the medium has in some way connected with the spirit of the deceased. Whilst this is all well and good for them, there are those who would disagree with this preconception of communication with the spirit world. The medium could, they say, be using other means in order to envisage the image of the once living that the recipient has on their person. This was the doubt that Vice Admiral Usborne Moore had to dispel when the

Bangs sisters were reading for him – that they were not copying the photograph in his inside pocket. (See Chapter Five.)

The common method today of producing a photograph on a mobile 'phone as evidence supporting a spirit drawing may equally be a cause for concern. Could the medium have seen the photograph before the event, either by chance or fraudulently? Those spirit artists whom I have known or interviewed would certainly not think about doing this since their entire reputation as medium and artist would then be in doubt (and the chances of discovery would be quite high).

Another theory offered by parapsychologists is that the spirit artist may have the ability to 'remote view' or have acute telepathic powers. Such abilities would be pretty remarkable in themselves – but not evidence of communication with the spirit world.

I have even heard other sceptics say, perhaps in desperation, that the spirit artist begins to draw a somewhat generic portrait while listening for a gasp of potential recognition in the audience, and then leads the recipient by questioning them. It just doesn't happen; in any case, it would be very difficult to know the difference between a gasp of emotional recognition of a loved one and a fake gasp or other similar cue.

There are those who believe and those who don't, and this is the conundrum for spirit art. Experienced spirit artists believe that they are working with the spirit world in order to produce this form of art. Yet we must admit that we do not know for sure how the creation of the art actually occurs when it is recognised. There has to be humility on the part of the artist. We believe that the art is a continuation of spiritual energy from another world that is experienced with love. Outside the religious constraints of Spiritualism, photographic evidence may not be necessary as evidence for who or what Spirit has produced; we know who our loved ones are, so that should just be enough.

Prior to the twenty-first century, portraits from demonstrations of spirit art were taken home by recipients who may not have been able to identify the deceased subject due to a lack of knowledge about the person other than their name. They might have been a rather distant relative or friend. Even so, there have been many cases where once the drawing has been seen later by a family or friend absent from the demonstration, recognition of the deceased occurs. Indeed, one of my own portraits took fifteen years to be recognised, when the recipient received photographs from Australia after the death of a grandfather they had never met! Once drawing and photograph were put together, there was no doubt that the image matched the drawing. As an artist and medium, acceptance of my drawings is vital to my reputation; if drawings are not recognised, I would be concerned that I am not creating what I say I am.

There is no known evidence of spirit drawings or paintings being created through *physical* mediumship since 1920. Contemporary spirit art is created through the supernatural processes of mental mediumship, in a similar manner to Frank Leah's drawings, whereby a medium detects a spirit entity by paranormal seeing, sensing (emotionally and physically) or hearing descriptions of the deceased. The terms for these sensations are clairvoyance, clairsentience and clairaudience. For example, Leah would see or sense the deceased before he drew the portrait; Coral Polge sensed the weight, height, colour of eyes, type of skin and clothes.

How can one sense a red beard or a dark skin colour or the age of the spirit? Well,to me, form, age and colour have subtle, etheric vibrations; for example, I feel the texture of the beard on my face, I sense the vibration of colour and the age of the person on my own physical body (more fully explained in my book *Portraits from Spirit*). Like the artist Paul Klee (1906-1940), who saw colour and shapes when hearing music (synaesthesia), I often sense colours when meeting people that I interpret as an indication of their state of health. (This is inherited from my mother, a hospital ward Sister during World War II in London and then in Liverpool. She was often asked by doctors to diagnose patients and was apparently always completely correct.)

The methods that other artists have used will be described in this chapter, each working differently just as traditional artists would. They have their own preference in terms of style, the materials they use, how they have developed their methods of connecting with the supernatural forces and how they approach their work.

The artists represented here have, each in their own way, pushed the boundaries of spirit art rather than copy the style of those before them or their contemporaries.

One of the most well-known of the contemporary spirit artists is Alan Stuttle who has become a major spiritualist figure in England and Europe since 1989. His work is not in fact any different or better than others' but he is the first in time order to work as a spirit artist after being trained by Coral Polge.

I have chosen Alan to begin this last collection of artists so that a comparison can be forged between his work and that of his American counterparts Susan Barnes – artist, lecturer and author, SNU award holder and art collector – and Joe Shiel, artist and lecturer. They both work in the area of Lily Dale, USA, and are tutors who pass their knowledge on for others to work with.

Following these are artists and non-artists who have created spirit art in different and exciting forms. Erika Andreasson draws "as though blind"; artist Josie Hutchinson works with the medium Joe Wilcox; Paul Clarke brings the spirit back to life as an animation; Saleire creates portraits digitally on a computer. These innovators make spirit impressions in and of the twenty-first century. There are many other very competent spirit artists who work and tutor others but the reason I have chosen these few is because their work is very different in both process and technique from the first simple automated drawings and paintings produced in the Victorian era; they have pushed the boundaries with their art and mediumship techniques.

Alan Stuttle, Susan Barnes and Joe Shiel

Alan Stuttle has created spirit art since Coral Polge's death in 2001. A spirit art lecturer at the Arthur Findlay College and the Lynwood Fellowship in Britain, he is an artist in his own right and an accredited member of the Royal Academy of Arts in London. He studied spirit art with Coral Polge, learning how to create spirit portraits, and attended lectures and courses at the Arthur Findlay College in order to gain experience of spirit portraiture as well as of psychic drawing and painting.

Meeting Alan at his gallery and studio in Scarborough, Yorkshire, he remarked that his actual occupation was that of a working artist "eking out a living from commissions" rather than as a spirit artist. While completing a triptych of war veterans in 2012, he said that he works psychically when he creates spirit portraiture but not when he creates his own artwork. Spirit portraits arise from the supernatural sensations that occur to him once he picks up the pencil or pastel, but this does not happen when he works on normal portraits or landscapes.

In his book, *The Spirit Artist*[58] he sets out a description of the conditions under which he works and advises his students to do the same, impressing his view of Spirit that the challenge, when creating spirit art, is with the person, not with the process; that is, with the artist and not with spirit helpers. He infers that spirit drawings and paintings are created by the person holding the pencil or brush *with the help of spirit* and not the other way

---

[58] *The Spirit Artist* (Stuttle A, lulu.com, 2015)

round. This is a different view to that of the pioneer Victorian artist Georgiana Houghton, who maintained that her hand had no part in the making of her paintings. We have seen that Coral Polge also said that her spirit guide drew the pictures. Perhaps if the drawings are recognised and can be shown to be evidence of a discarnate spirit surviving death, then the manner of drawing does not matter.

Alan Stuttle creates his spirit portraits at an easel with ordinary artists' materials, charcoal and pastel, usually working on paper. He does not create spirit art in his studio with oils on canvas, he only creates them during public performances, demonstrations and private readings. He has often been invited to draw spirit portraits in Europe at spiritualist meetings, where he sketches in front of large audiences and usually works with a medium such as his partner Jan Elliot; she attunes to the spirit communicators and gives verbal information about the spirit's life as Alan draws. These demonstrations are made in conjunction with an interpreter who relays the information about the portrait to the audience.

While visiting the Arthur Findlay College, I asked Alan if he would create a spirit portrait for me; I wanted to see who the spirit was helping me to draw supernaturally. Three pastel sketches were made by him during this private reading. It was held in one of the Arthur Findlay College's teaching workrooms on the top floor of the building and lasted for about an hour. He had his easel already set up in the room with pastels on a small table. He asked me to sit at a chair beside him so that he could "sense the energy field". During the reading Alan said he linked into the energies surrounding me before he had begun to draw. I did not feel him do this; indeed, his actions seemed reminiscent of an artist simply sketching from life, taking an occasional look at me to check for something as a part of his drawing. He was not looking directly at me but at the energies surrounding my body.

Like other spirit artists, the method he used to obtain a spirit portrait is unique to him. To begin, he asked if I would like to choose three colours from his pastels box so I chose blue, green and yellow whilst he chose a neutral skin tone. He smudged these colours onto the Ingres paper already mounted on his easel. The chosen colours were interpreted spiritually as he 'sensed their vibrations', each one meaning something different in relation to my energy field. Having explained each colour, he began to create the central portrait and then, by moving across from the smudged colours, he sketched four more faces.

These portraits contained spiritual evidence, as did the further portraits he drew above the main image of a lady. Once the major portrait was completed, Alan explained that he was working 'psychically' when describing what the colours meant and 'spiritually' when creating the portraits. He also reported that he began to sense the energy of the spirit people psychically after linking into my energies, which enabled him to draw the series of portraits illustrated.

Alan had created a lovely and professionally drawn sketch. However, sadly, I didn't recognise any of the portraits at the time and could not immediately say that the people were of my family. From a book *Common Ancestors* written by my cousin Allan Carter, I knew my great-grandfather was a Church of England minister and that his daughters were named Lily and Daisy; but, as I have said, I did not recognise the portraits in the picture at the time – that is until 2016, about ten years later.

On looking again at the drawing, there were details catching my eye that were also in some photographs I had found: the chain and locket around great-aunt Lily's neck and the style of her hair. There is an early twentieth century photograph of my mother's family in my book *Portraits from Spirit*. When I looked through my book, I realised that Alan's portrait of the main female character was wearing a chain around her neck with her hair set in the uncommon way, just as illustrated in the drawing. I placed the two images together and found a strong similarity between the woman to the lower right in the photograph and Alan's portrait.

Although the church minister in his drawing did not look like my relative, it is interesting that he drew the minister alongside a figure that I now recognise as my great-aunt. Not having been born when the photograph was taken, I would have had no recollection of these people.

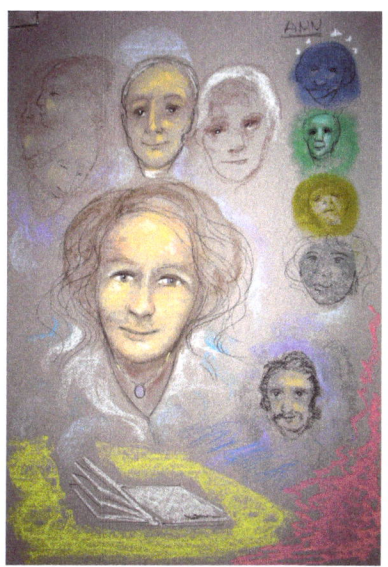 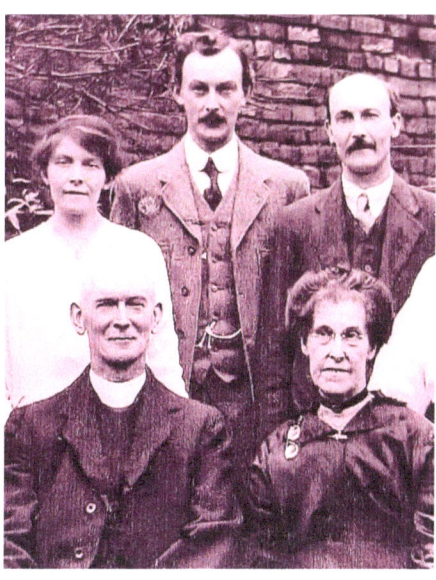

Great Aunt Lily and Family   *Photograph of Great Aunt Lily (lower right)*

Alan Stuttle agrees that sometimes a portrait may not be recognised: "At the end of a demonstration, those who have been contacted can collect a drawing. That in itself is satisfying, but if at a later date the recipient produces a photograph of the person drawn, the satisfaction is even greater. During the session a recipient may fail to understand or accept what is being said [or drawn]."

During public demonstrations, Stuttle often added familial objects and landscapes into his spirit artwork. At such an event at the Arthur Findlay Centre (now the Barbanell Centre) in Stafford, UK, in 2014, he drew a portrait with his back to the audience so he could not see the recipient, while his partner Jan gave her impressions regarding the picture. According to the man who recognised the image, this representation of the deceased was accurate.

But the portrait also illustrated a place in time and included objects known to have belonged to the deceased, which the recipient said he recognised. The impression of a church in the background of the drawing was a clue, said by the recipient to be the one where the deceased had been married. The medals drawn to the side had been earned by the person in the war. Cherry blossoms in bloom were also pictured, but not yet in leaf, which Alan remarked, "indicated the time of year that the person died." The addition of these familial objects (like the chain and locket in my own portrait), seem to produce a memory link for the recipient of the painting, enabling it to be more easily recognised.

Thus, unlike previous spirit artists, Alan Stuttle's portraits *tell a story*. The inclusion of these objects and landscapes relating to the deceased, the everyday symbols of flowers and objects or specific belongings, acts as tools to trigger memories for the recipient to recognise. Each image reveals a story about the life of the deceased. By recreating art from what Alan believes to be supernatural etheric sensations, the recipient of the drawing agrees or disagrees with his remarks, all of which builds upon the story of the deceased for the medium.

Alan defines the process of visually representing memories through reliving the past as art, saying, "Memories remain with you [when deceased]… but are drawn through the artist." We can see that the non-visual and non-aural supernatural impressions he receives and then draws due to his "tapping into the cosmic forces of the universe", give hope that an afterlife is real.

Two other spirit artists who work in a similar manner to Stuttle are the Americans Joe Shiel and Susan Barnes, both also trained artists who once lived and worked at the Lily Dale Assembly, New York.

They too create evidential spirit portraits during private sittings and public demonstrations, yet their artwork is very different in technique to Alan's and also to each other's.

Like Frank Leah, Joe produces portraits of the spirits of the deceased without having met the recipients in life, whereas Susan interprets the feelings and sensations she receives from colours and symbols as she draws 'auragraphs' for a sitter, giving both psychic and spiritual evidence.

During an interview with Joe Shiel at his studio in 2014, he told me that he is a spiritualist minister although he had been raised a Roman Catholic in Massachusetts, New England. In a similar manner to that of Stuttle, Joe receives extrasensory perceptions before he draws the picture.

"[My] first inspired art [was] from the age of five," he said. "I drew eleven people when the house was full up with priests and nuns. After that, because the dexterity of my eye-to-hand co-ordination was beyond that of a five year-old… they [the Catholic Church] didn't understand how I could draw like that well… [I] probably drew back then as well as I do now, maybe better. I named all eleven people in the picture.

"I had a spiritual calling to be a Jesuit priest; I thought what was happening to me was a spiritual experience of some sort. Back then I couldn't have explained that to you for all the tea in China.

"I was drawing pictures, just doodling people in the library, and on more than one occasion I had people come by and say things like, "That's my uncle." I had no possession, it was just a doodle, but that's how I got started. I didn't know what I was doing. I had no idea what I had, no idea of mediumship, you know, if you had told me to go to a psychic I would have told you to go somewhere else, I had no idea of it [twenty years ago]."

From these beginnings, he decided that his artwork was not controlled by 'spirit forces' but by sensations that he experienced in his body as he drew. He demonstrated this by showing me a representation of one of his drawings of both human and animal faces. This illustration was one of Joe's first impressions of these extrasensory, paranormal sensations. He said of this painting, "It is a mixture of faces, so this is how I started out, I started by doing what I call multiple drawings… and these drawings were recognised." The recipient of the portrait recognised the depiction of a red-capped young man in the illustration; houses, horses, cars and trees were also included as spirit memories, giving evidence of the hobbies enjoyed by the young man as well as a sense of place in his life.

His more recent spirit portraiture reveals that, like other spirit artists before him, the images he creates resemble pre-mortem memory photographs of loved ones that are often recognised and almost identical to the photograph. One such pencil portrait, for example, was confirmed to be that of a young woman's deceased father. She wrote to Joe later, "Thank you again for… connecting with my father. This was an amazing experience and has brought some happiness back into my life… a gift I will never forget." The untitled drawing had meant nothing to Joe until it was placed next to a photograph on the young woman's iPhone, when the resemblance between the two was clear. This, as in the case of Hollie, is the beginning of the use of modern technology as evidence for the deceased.

Another of Joe's spirit drawings is that of a very kindly-looking woman. This is a portrait that typifies the evidential qualities of spirit art. The drawing and portrait are extremely close in identity, especially the manner in which the portrait demonstrates emotional qualities of the woman. Here we feel as though we know her. The drawing of a woman unknown to the artist is not copied from the identifying photograph but has similar traits: the loving look in the eyes, the smile, the manner in which the spirit sits, are all qualities an artist when drawing a model from life would wish to create in a drawing. The earrings and brooch would also support identification for the recipient of the picture. We, as onlookers, may have the idea that the artist knows exactly what they are doing when they create an image such as this, but often they have no idea of the outcome of their work when they begin the drawing.

Joe Shiel explains his thoughts on mind, spirit, process and materials in this way:

"I think the mind and the heart determine how I am going to work. I think the [art] medium has nothing to do with it except it is there. If I wanted to do it… run my fingers through the sand and that's all I had to do it with, that's what I would [draw] it with… I can't say that the pencil itself determines anything, or the chalk, or even the oils, although I love the oils because of the richness of the feel of working with them… I have a friend who does spiritual art, not spirit art, but spiritual art, and when he took a year off just painting in his house… he ran out of paint… and used coffee. It's like I feel the same way, it's whatever I've got, I'd cut the carpet up to look like your grandmother if I had to."

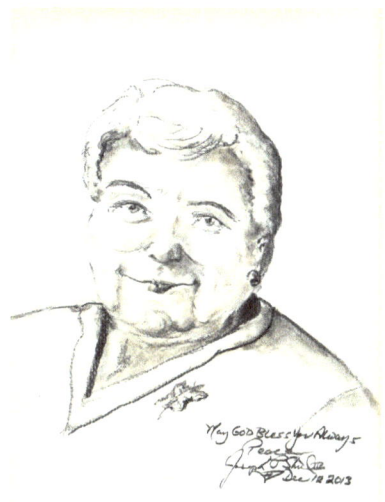
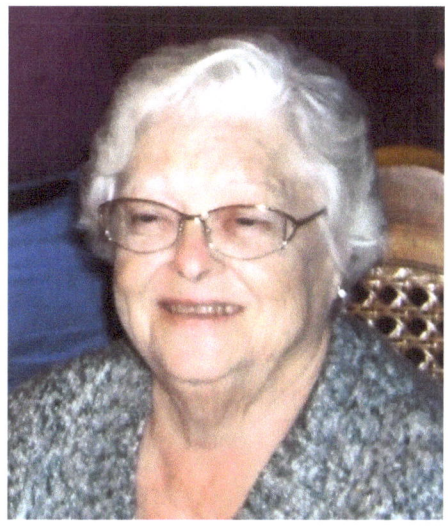

Woman   *Photograph of 'Woman'*

Whilst he believes 'spirit art' and 'spiritual art' are different, Joe Shiel also proposes that the art can be created from anything and that as he develops, whatever art he creates, there is always some form of spirituality in it. Here we have the notion of *spirituality*, as distinct from the human spirit, emerging as another aspect of the art. Shiel was one of the first of the spirit artists to speak of the presence of spirituality in his art. In future interviews with other British artists this is non-existent, as though there may be more freedom of thought in American spirit art than in the UK.

Fellow American and British-trained spirit artist, Dr Susan B Barnes, is also a spirit artist and spiritualist tutor. Susan's interest in spirit art began in 2006 and within nine years she had been certified as a medium and speaker by the Spiritualists' National Union. As a regular visitor to the Arthur Findlay College and to the Barbanell Centre in Stafford, she found that training there aided her natural abilities as a medium and an artist. She also attended workshops and training sessions run by Alan Stuttle. Susan is an academic and forward-thinking student of mediumship (who has also gained a PhD in Media Ecology).

"I think I have been doing [mediumship] much longer than I ever imagined," she told me. "I mean, I didn't think of it as spirit art. I always knew I had mediumistic tendencies and knew I had psychic abilities throughout my life. But when I started to do different types of pictures, I chose to try to do a juxtaposition between advertising images – because they represent current iconic imageries to me – with classical ones, and what I wasn't totally aware of was that I was actually drawing past-life pictures. I mean, I was trained at Pratt [the Pratt Institute School of Art, New York City] and so in my undergraduate work, although multimedia, I majored in fine arts while I was there. I did have a career as a graphic designer for a while before I got into teaching advertising as a professor."

Whilst Susan, like Alan Stuttle and myself, is a qualified art teacher, her spirit artwork developed outside her professional work. She is now recognised as the one of the few SNU certified mediums in the USA and, unlike other spirit art tutors, her spiritual work includes the role of a collector or curator as she exhibits her own spirit artwork alongside that of other artists at her galleries in Lily Dale and Fredonia, New York State.

"I started saving all the work and didn't throw any of it away – gradually I came to have a collection of all kinds of different spirit art and, when I started putting the collection together, then I realised that some of my own art fitted in with the spirit-inspired work."

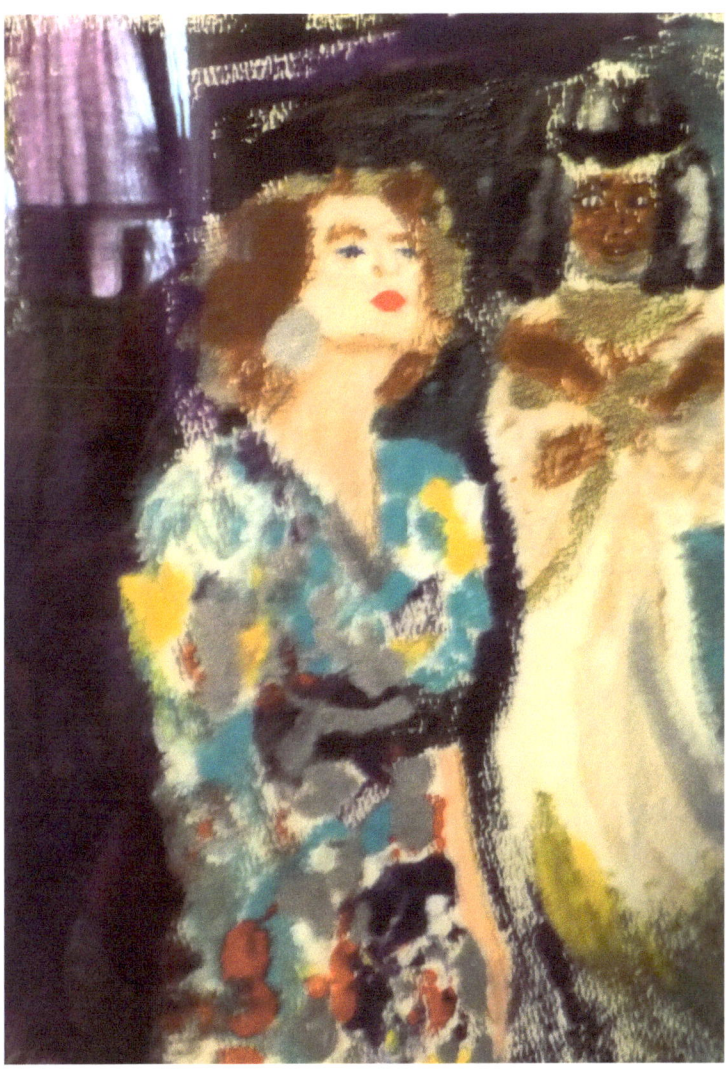

Egypt

Illustrated in her piece *Egypt* here, she considers elements of both spirit and spirituality. Although the concept of spirit guides is not truly defined within spiritualist philosophy – because drawings of, for example, American Indians and Egyptian priests cannot be proven – they help students understand the difference between evidential and non-evidential art. Susan's watercolour painting is suggestive of what mediums call communication with their spirit guide.

Such guides, as mentioned earlier when explaining the work of Coral Polge, are believed to give spiritual direction to the medium or artist. In Susan's image, the figure to the right demonstrates a supporting role as the medium works; each figure is represented as separate, in their own space and time, yet continuously in communication with the medium. This image is reminiscent of the work of the Victorian artist, Anna Mary Howitt, with Barnes' painting representing a call for spiritual help or guidance from the other world.

"I think that a difference between the English spirit art and the American," she says, "is that in England everybody is so focused on evidence that this shapes the way they think about spirit art. Whereas here in America we are not as concerned, we are more interested in the messages in many ways more than evidence, so that people, when they do the art, can express their feelings more."

As an art collector, she attended a public demonstration by trance artist José Medrado and successfully bid for the painting *Ida* that included the signature of Renoir (see Chapter Three). She watched the painting develop under his fingers while he appeared to be in an altered state of consciousness. To Susan, the painting of a red-haired lady had a strong likeness to her own red-haired grandmother. She believes now that, while José was in trance, Renoir completed the painting in the shape and form of her grandmother. Thus José was not only painting 'under the control of Renoir' but was also creating an evidential image of a family member.

"I was in the back of the room but could see because there was a projector there. He blobs the paint down and then he starts working with it. The amazing thing for me is how the colours don't blend together because the way he works [the paint] should all be brown and mashed into and it doesn't, it doesn't… he did the background first and the last thing he did was the face, and it's funny, he likes to paint redheads 'cause I guess Renoir did it too, but my grandmother was a redhead and she had green eyes and he's got very distinctly green eyes in the portrait… People have said it looks like me, which is true because I look like my grandmother."

Susan Barnes did not hesitate to say that she recognised the portrait, repeating this point several times during our interview and with a tone of astonishment in her voice at having received an evidential painting from 'Renoir'. It is unusual for José to create an evidential portrait, since many of his quasi-Expressionist paintings are representational of many deceased famous artists' work. In Susan's painting, however, we appear to have an exception to the rule: the image looks like her grandmother.

By visiting demonstrations of mediumship in both America and Britain, Susan has amassed a collection of spirit artwork, mainly evidential spirit portraiture and auragraphs, which are psychic in concept. With a love of curation, she hopes ultimately to have as many spirit artists exhibiting in her galleries as possible, thereby demonstrating the worth of the art to both spiritualists and 'outsiders'.

Although contemporary evidential spirit art appears to be a continuation of the work of Frank Leah, Coral Polge, Alan Stuttle and others, there are those who are neither mediums nor artists yet who create spirit portraiture in very different ways from their forebears. For example, there is Erika Andreasson, an untrained artist. Also important are the artist Josie Hutchinson, a non-medium, working with the medium Joe Wilcox, a non-artist, who perform together in order to produce art and evidence of life after death.

Erika Andreasson, Josie Hutchinson and Joe Wilcox

Living in Europe, Erika Andreasson is still a product of the British training of spirit artists. She was born in Boras, Sweden, and is a healer who now teaches classes in mediumship in her home town. Like others, Erika came to create spirit art after she had attended a course at the Arthur Findlay College in the UK. She is one of only a few European spirit artists, but is not a trained artist and is one of the most inexperienced of the figures discussed here.

Relying solely on her spiritual intuition, she creates her images in an unusual manner by drawing "as though blind". Her portraits in pencil, crayon or pastel are produced in the dark, yet her illustrations of the deceased are surprisingly accurate given that she does not see what she is drawing. She says of this work, "This portrait is done in darkness. I couldn't see my hand or how it sketched. It took about five minutes..."[59]

At first, she would allow her hand to move where it was prompted to go, producing clear drawings. She did not know about the automatic art of Anna Mary Howitt and Georgiana Houghton, and of how they drew in the dark, so it is interesting that her work shows similar signs of development between the early and later illustrations in the history of spirit art and artists. Once she had experienced that the portraits could be recognised, especially with the use of colour, each now supports the evidential theme. Further, by drawing familial objects into the pictures such as glasses, eye and skin colour, earrings and clothes, the recipient is more easily able to recognise the deceased as a drawing when corresponding to a photograph.

Another image was originally chosen to illustrate Erika's artwork that was withdrawn by request due to the sadness the image held for the recipient. Allowing us to reproduce a different image, Erika helps us to understand that these spirit drawings hold such deep emotions and memories of those who have passed to Spirit that to see them again sometimes does not offer comfort to the bereaved; and so the family member of Yngve offered this image

---

[59] Erika Andreasson placed this image, with others, on her Facebook page in 2013: https://www.facebook.com/erika.andreasson.50?fref=ts

to help others understand the emotions attached to owning a spirit drawing or painting. As each image unfolds the story of the deceased person, each recipient can hold an image of their loved one, a treasure in itself. Each artist, each spirit portrait, each recipient has a story to be told, and for us here creating the history of such a mastery we begin to understand how, to spiritualists, spirit art is so important.

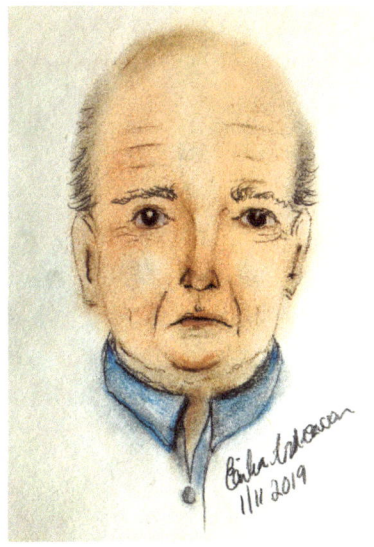

Yngve

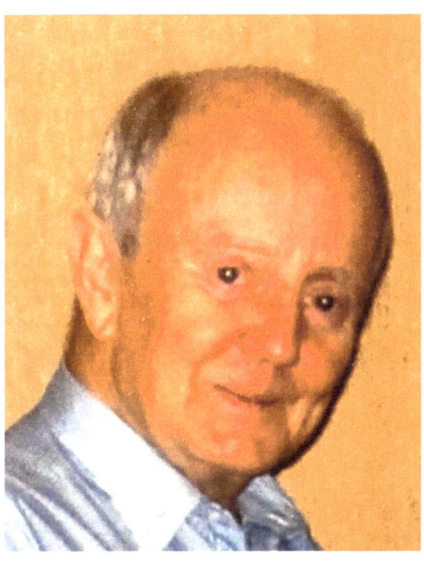

Photograph of Yngve

Many contemporary spirit artists work alone but there is an alternative to this, by sharing the demonstration between two people, an artist and a medium. The artist creates spirit images on their own and the medium relays a message. Thus two sensitives, an artist and a medium, can combine their skills and work together. Indeed, there are some artists who prefer to work with a medium during large demonstrations of spirit art. Alan Stuttle works with his partner Jan, the medium, and I myself supported the late Liverpool medium Tommy Richardson, which worked very well. There are two methods when artist and medium individually create image and message. They can separately identify the same spirit person; alternatively the artist works alone, with the medium making a link with the drawing once it is completed.

One of today's such alliances is between the artist Josie Hutchinson and the medium Joe Wilcox. Whilst there are other mediums and artists who work together, it is unusual for an artist who is not a medium to produce spirit drawings alone. Josie says that she "sees or senses the impression of a person in spirit before and during the public demonstration" and is able to interpret through these senses the spirit people whom she proceeds to draw. But she does not think of herself as a medium. During a demonstration she sits behind Joe Wilcox and quietly draws in coloured pencils while he attempts to make a link with the portrait in order to receive a verbal message from the spirit world.

"No-one can teach you how to attune to spirit people," says Joe, explaining the process at an evening demonstration. "How can you attune to [Spirit] when you don't know where they are and you don't know who they are? What you do is make your mind passive and receptive and then they come…

"Now… you see Josie with some really nice stories [portraits], very distinctive, she doesn't like to stand up and talk, so that's my job." Sometimes, drawings are done in advance of a public meeting, "…so I have to play catch-up before we know who [in Spirit] was going to be present…"

When Josie completes a drawing, Joe begins to 'read' it by gathering sensations from the spirit who has been drawn. As he studies the drawing, he speaks to the audience, relaying the information he receives from his communicators and asking the audience to speak to him if they recognise any of his information or the drawing. While Joe speaks, Josie continues to draw portraits, producing five or six images during a demonstration.

During the demonstration I observed, Josie had created a drawing three days before our meeting in September, 2014. This portrait was recognised as that of a deceased work colleague by a person in the audience. The recipient did not want to be identified here but gave permission for the circumstances by which the image was drawn, read and accepted to be described.

The recipient was unable formally to validate the likeness of her work colleague with a photograph because he had died thirty years earlier and no photograph was available. This did not appear to be a problem for Josie or Joe since they continued with their work after the drawing had been recognised and accepted. Some may consider that this dual technique does not have quite the same positive reinforcement as portraits created by a mediumistic artist alone; nevertheless, this form of art offers convincing evidence to a recipient.

Saleire and Paul Clarke

Other contemporary artists are the pioneers of new and exciting ways to produce spirit art, using digital means. Retired art lecturer Paul Clarke and spiritual healer Saleire (Sally) Tracy both digitalise their spiritualistic impressions on computers. Non-artist Saleire creates her portraits using a computer alone whilst animator Paul draws a portrait and then proceeds to make the image 'come back to life'!

Thus, in taking creativity beyond the confines of a religious belief structure, spirit art is being altered and new techniques herald an era of change. Saleire and Paul do not know one another and yet they are two inspired creators of unique contemporary spirit art processes. Their innovative ideas show that the spirit art movement is strengthening beyond its past inherent belief structure towards a new art form.

Saleire admits that she "cannot draw at all" with a pencil but found that, by working on a computer, "the spirit world took over" and she developed a form of spirit art that no-one else has replicated. I found Saleire's work on Facebook and was drawn to her spirit impressions because they were different to any other spirit portraits

I had seen. A spiritual healer, she has little art training and began producing spirit portraiture using computer graphics because she realised that her drawing skills were inadequate. She works very quickly on the computer, using a Bamboo Tablet with Photoshop to draw the spirit impressions she receives. She feels that she herself doesn't draw the portrait: it is drawn for her as though she is being controlled – that is, not just her hand but also the computer itself.

She showed me her self-portrait online. Here the digital image appeared to enhance a sense of her presence, of her innermost spirit. This seemed to make her work different in comparison with earlier pencil or pastel portraits from other artists. It may be suggested that a self-portrait cannot truly be said to be spirit art. Nevertheless, the portrait has a life of its own, something extra, with the smile reflected in the eyes. Previous spirit portraits, although competent, have often appeared vacant as though the spirit had left and just an outer shell remained. In her portrait there is a genuine sense of something else within the image, a numinous presence suggestive of a spiritual force.

She informed me that at times, when she first began, she tried to enhance her drawing skills by copying paintings produced by the Masters, but does not think of them as spirit guides in the same way that Coral Polge did. For example, she produced a digitalised drawing of the oil painting *Portrait of a Woman* (c.1430), attributed to the Flanders artist, Robert Campin (c.1375-1444). Whilst clarity of painting is inherent in Campin's painting, his image reflects a younger and softer persona in comparison with Saleire's, perhaps because the eyes are downward cast with the mouth held serenely. Her illustration differentiated itself from the original by digital clarity. According to art historian Wendy Beckett, Campin's original illustrates "the individuality of the sitter"; is Beckett alluding to the *spirit* of the sitter, as Saleire's rendition does?[60]

---

[60] *The Story of Painting: The Essential Guide to the History of Western Art* (Sr W Beckett, Dorling Kindersley Publishers Ltd, 1994)

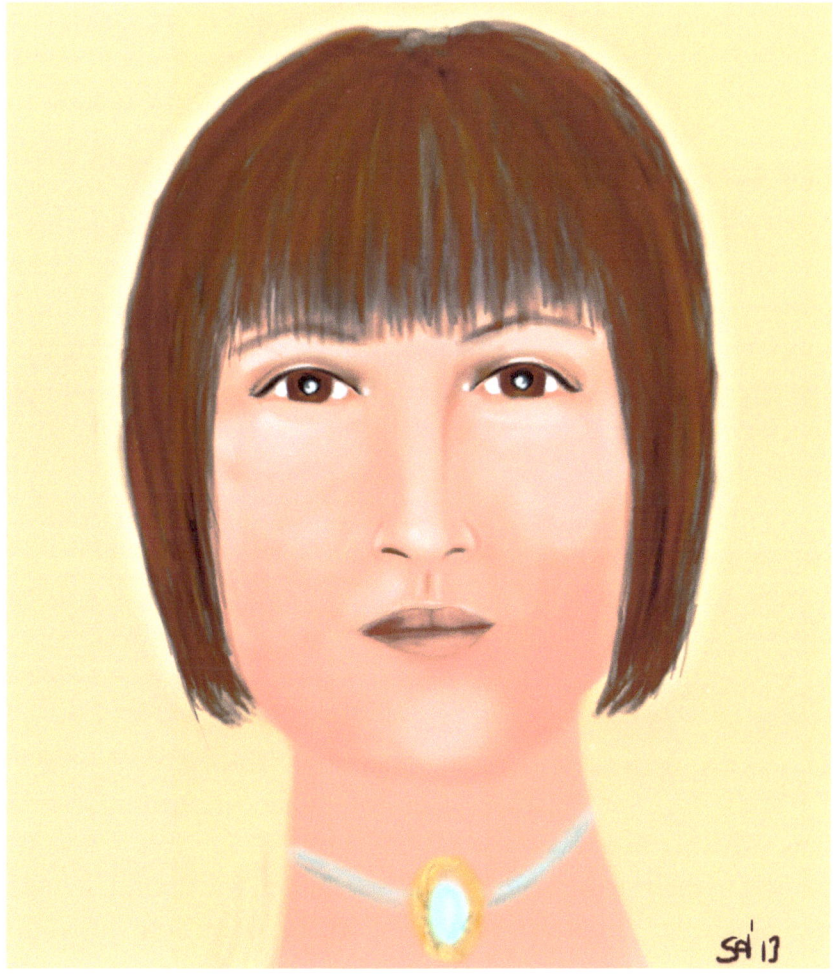

Julie

Be this as it may, when creating spirit portraiture and not copying others' work, Saleire is able to reproduce on her computer the essence of the person that she senses, the individuality of the spirit. During my telephone interview with her, she drew a portrait on her tablet that I could certainly verify as a likeness to an art student whom I taught in the early 1980s. The student, Julie, whom I had taught forty years previously when Head of Art at a small high school in Liverpool, had been seventeen years old with dark auburn hair, which is represented in the image as are the innate qualities of the girl I knew. I do not have a photograph of her yet I clearly remember Julie as being shy and with a gentle sadness in her eyes. Of course, I cannot identify the jewellery at her neck but Julie had died suddenly by choking, perhaps signified by Saleire's drawing of a choker, a fashion item popular in the 1980s.

This digitally created spirit portrait captures an essence of the presence of this quiet, unassuming personality and of her innermost spirit. Thus, Saleire's portraits created on the computer appear to present both a pre-mortem image as well as the essence of the person's spirit. As a healer, she feels that she heals the soul through her work.

"All I want to do," she says, "is share my experiences of these beings of light with those that are experiencing the same thing. If they match up with yours, that's great, and if they don't, that's great too as it shows their immense capacity to communicate in whatever way we are able to comprehend." As a person who is very sensitive to the earthly and spirit worlds, she shares her knowledge with those who seek their own truth.

She works alone but little is known of her background. Being very private and leading a quiet life, she does not call people to her but suggests that when people are ready they will find her, as I did. She believes that she is here to show that there is not just 'one true answer' to life in the mortal body, or even one truth, rather to demonstrate quietly that we can receive answers, but these can only be based on the information we are able to understand at the time.

Saleire had been seeing spiritual beings most of her life, but only around 2013 did she begin to draw them. As her image of my deceased student shows, she is very capable of linking with the spirit world and creates her art as though the student were in the room with her. Her method is in some way not unlike that of Frank Leah, but she works totally digitally, unable to draw except on a computer when the urge takes her.

As a true innovator of digital spirit art, and not willing to place herself in the limelight, she is to be acclaimed for moving spirit art into the digital and contemporary world.

Paul Clarke, on the other hand, is a trained artist and lecturer who, after studying spirit art, had the idea of creating animations of his portraits of the deceased. He was easily able to produce recognisable and evidential drawings of the deceased, but his inventive mind took him further, imaginatively recreating the spirit drawing as a digitalised animation.

When I asked Paul whether he was clairvoyant, clairsentient or clairaudient, he said, "I don't know what I am doing 'alf the time… I just do it." Later, recounting the time he had spent at the Arthur Findlay College being taught mediumship by Alan Stuttle and other tutors, he said he still doesn't understand "what [linking with Spirit] is all about." For him, this knowledge does not really matter because he is able to create spirit portraits without that information.

Although I did not meet Paul until he arrived in my Spirit Art classroom in early 2000 at the then Arthur Findlay Centre (now the Barbanell Centre), Stafford, it turned out that we had both taught art in separate secondary schools in Toxteth, Liverpool, within a quarter of a mile of one another almost three decades earlier. He is from Lancashire himself and had begun teaching in Liverpool in the late 1960s, knowing several of the art teachers that I knew (since I had been Chair of the Liverpool Art Teachers' Society). He had then moved to the Midlands, teaching art.

During his time under my tutelage, I gave him the opportunity to demonstrate spirit art on the platform, giving messages to an audience. His portraiture was the best of all my students but he still required understanding of how the spirit world worked with him. Since then he has worked with several mediums, such as the West Midlands trance medium, Sheila Green.

Unlike Saleire, Paul is a trained artist and clearly able to recreate the physical presence of a person; like Alan Stuttle, Frank Leah and Coral Polge, he has transferred his drawing training to the creation of recognisable faces of the deceased. His spirit drawings appear to have a life of their own.

In 2013, he drew the spirit portrait of young man whom I recognised. Yet this drawing demonstrated that even though a photograph of the subject may not appear similar, as Frank Leah's drawings of Spirit did, the portrait nevertheless acknowledged the man as just before he died. This man, 'S', was ill-at-ease with himself, an alcoholic and working as a musician, and it was certainly the same man in the sketch as in the photograph. As with Saleire's interpretations, Clarke's work illustrated what he sensed, the sadness of the man. This is a new approach – drawing the spirit or persona of a subject as they were while living.

Paul suggested that he drew the spirit "without thinking", allowing his hand to move of its own accord, as other contemporary artists have described the process. He also admitted that when a person recognised one of the spirit portraits he created he was overwhelmed, inferring that although he believed in the existence of the spirit world, he was surprised when the drawing was identified by someone he does not know.

Shown here is a colour photocopy of another of Paul's subjects, *Alan*. Unlike previous spirit artists, Paul had copies made of his drawings so that he could keep the originals. Normally, a spirit artist will give the original work to the recipient but Paul, exerting his right as an artist, protects his copyright in the case of spirit art.

Paul became frustrated by the fact that his impressions were static, as an illustration of one moment in time. As an animator, he felt that his spirit portraits needed to move, to 'come back to life', so he began working on a project enabling the spirits to have presence.

He demonstrated this new art to me with a spirit image of his dearly loved deceased mother, drawn from memory, making the image move. By manually tracing his initial drawing, a basic cartoon was made and then Paul drew five or six more images with the head in different positions, recreating the one image into several separate and different images. These were then photographed in sequence, thus animating the movement of his mother's head and 'bringing her back to life' as a moving spirit portrait.

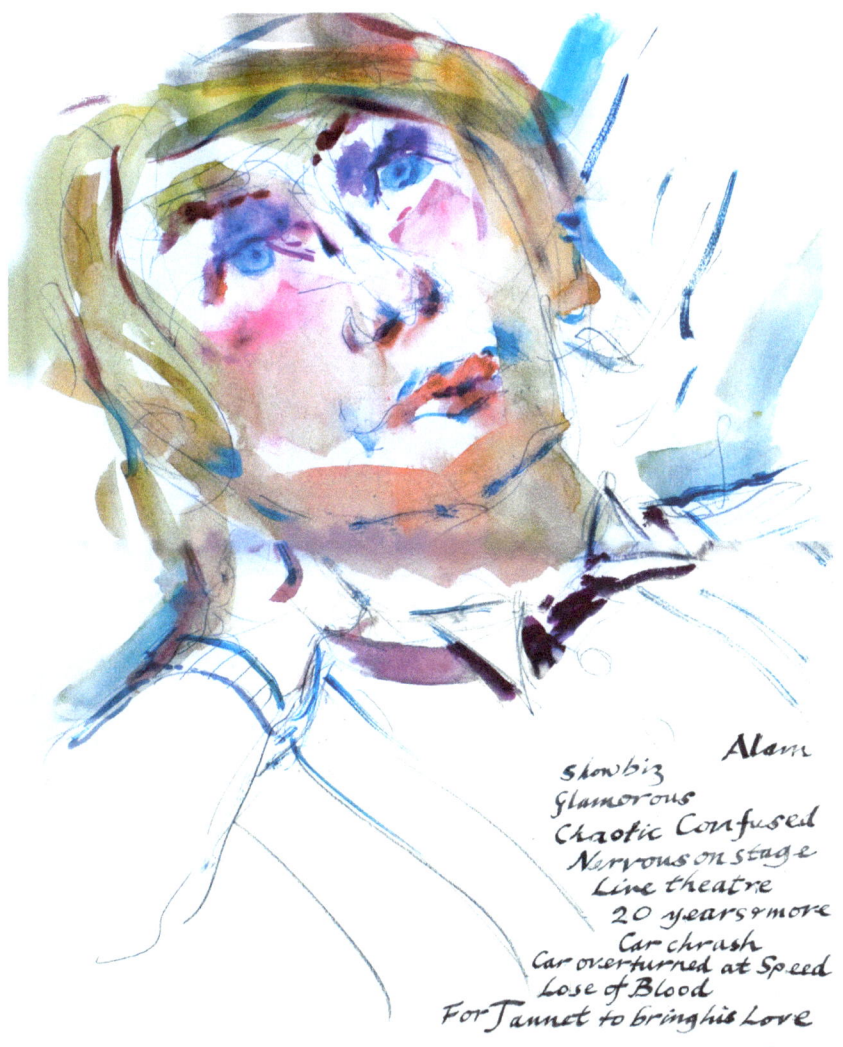

Alan

Paul had inadvertently created the next step in the development of spirit art as moving pictures of the spirit world. This is a new and completely innovative method of creating spirit portraits, solely Paul's idea, and it has changed the landscape of spirit art, giving the art itself new life by animating and energising spirit images so that they live again. Although most contemporary spirit artists still use the methods, processes, art materials and philosophies of the past, there is no waning of spirit art as a product. However, Paul Clarke and Saleire, by using spirit art skills in combination with modern digital technology, have developed a new genre within the canon.

Spirit art now seems to be an emerging art form in its own right. The highly criticised, abstracted spirit drawings and paintings of the Victorian era were dismissed by both conventional artists of the time and by critics. Then the non-abstracted Victorian British and American psychographic portrait drawings and the American precipitated paintings materialised as more evidential forms of spirit art. New contemporary forms of the genre have evolved and continue to do so today.

    These provide both spiritualists and the general public with a product that seems, on the surface at least, to offer proof that the quintessence, the spirit as presence, of a human or an animal survives the death of the physical body. The person post-life can be illustrated as a new art form and is totally recognisable. This century, spirit art does not have the same oppressive dictates surrounding its production of the Victorian and early twentieth century days. The art appears to have freed itself from these constraints and, in some ways, from Spiritualism as well.

REFLECTIONS

So here we have, at the moment, six classifications of spirit art over a timespan of some one hundred and seventy years. This is a movement that was almost halted by the major English art critic for the late nineteenth century, John Ruskin. He made judgements regarding what is 'good art' and what is the value of art itself. In this statement in *Modern Painters* (Volume 2, c.1856), Ruskin suggests the methods by which supernatural beings, or spirits, could manifest themselves and be drawn:

"There are four ways Beings supernatural may be conceived as manifesting themselves to human sense. The first, by external types, signs or influences… The second, by assuming of a form not properly belonging to them… The third, by the manifestation of a form properly belonging to them, but not necessarily seen… And the fourth, by their operation on the human form which they influence or inspire…"

There is a paradox here. Why, if he meant what he wrote, did Ruskin then discredit the influence and inspiration of the spirits on the artists?

He attempts to clarify how supernatural beings could be perceived by a spirit medium. However, he omits to say that a form of art was being created by those beings right under his nose – and by his friends – as drawings and paintings. Here, of course, Ruskin's experiences of the supernatural was naturally in line with his own experience as an artist, not as a medium, and with his belief in Christian dogma. He reasoned that there *are* spiritual or supernatural beings who could be drawn, but did not believe that a mortal artist was able to draw the deceased.

His opinion relied solely on what he knew and understood, rather than taking account of what spirit mediums told him. Spirit art, whilst supernatural in production, was not 'holy' in the Christian sense, therefore it was of no value to him. Being so influential, his pronouncements regarding Spiritualism and spirit art have strongly influenced the history of art, causing spirit art to be, in the main, blocked from the traditional canon and history of art.

On the other hand, the artist James Whistler together with the Pre-Raphaelite Brotherhood appears to have understood the value and meaning of spirit art created under the guidance of Spirit, as they sat in séance together with their friend and artist, Anna Mary Howitt. Whistler, using what he had witnessed in the séance room, also attempting to recreate the spirit or essence of the person in his somewhat etheric portrait paintings.

This is when spirit art could have taken off and into the art history books. But, because Ruskin was such a powerful figure in Victorian culture, and because artists needed to sell their paintings so that they would be remembered for their work, it didn't!

Apart from these six classifications of spirit art, there appears to be no other art form with similar supernatural production and creative properties in the history of art, making this movement unique. And from the dark séances of the Victorian era to the lightning-fast automatic drawings of the twenty-first century, spirit art is still moving on into the digital age.

One cannot help but wonder… could it be that the upcoming spirit world with its modern inhabitants will soon be able spontaneously to manipulate a computer mouse, or draw onto a tablet or mobile 'phone, without a living human being involved? We haven't heard of this yet, but watch this space as my generation become dust and the digitally savvy take our place in the world.

Spirit artists, like most people, often followed the religion of their upbringing and may have been Christian, for example, when young; but then they also joined spiritualist organisations such as the SNU. In this way they would train as mediums and spirit artists, creating work inspired by their conviction in a spirit world without the constraints of other organised belief structures. The social importance of having a traditional belief alongside Spiritualism began to change in the late twentieth century, when freedom of religious conviction became more easily tolerated by society.

The processes involved in the making of spirit art, on the other hand, began to change around the turn of the twenty-first century. The pioneers who had instigated this were Frank Leah and Coral Polge, whose work had a purpose, which made their art different from previous spirit art. They led the way for other creatives to follow. By developing artistic rigour alongside a belief in Spirit, they, perhaps unintentionally, reinvented spirit art as a product for spiritual evidence. For the first time, the *image* overrode the verbal message and became the primary communication between the two worlds of life and death. It was Frank and Coral who forged the way for the artists of today to use the photograph as visual evidence to support spiritualist philosophy.

Deliberate changes to the creative processes produced a transformation of the art. Contemporary mediumistic artists, building on the working knowledge and convictions of the past, converted their belief into paintings and drawings with methods that have moved the art forward. The teaching techniques and work created by these artists have attracted innovative ideas from trained artists, photographers and lecturers.

Those who were already formally trained artists or teachers, such as Alan Stuttle, Paul Clarke, Susan Barnes and Joe Shiel, were ready to make that change. There have been others who were not trained as artists but as mediums, such as Saleire, the author, artist and Irish poet Muriel Roberts, and the Swedish medium Erika

Andreasson. So it can be seen that being an artist has not made a difference to the evidential art created after the turn of the century. There are also mediums who are untrained in the techniques of art who work alongside artists as they create the drawings, paintings and animation.

The artists selected for this book are by no means a definitive group, nor have they been chosen because they have been in the public eye. But they have all developed unique and new forms of spirit art using previously unknown techniques. These people have taken the methods of automatism, trance, precipitated and psychographic techniques, evidential and now digital techniques step by step forward for the advancement of spiritual understanding.

A PERSONAL WORD BY THE PUBLISHER

When Ann Bridge Davies approached me with her wonderful manuscript, I had no idea of the extraordinary spiritual synchronicity that was to unfold.

Several decades before, I had visited a little-known spirit artist, John Cotton, as research for a degree thesis on Parapsychology. An unassuming retired civil servant and Church of England lay preacher, with no training in art whatsoever, John had one day found himself going into trance and later seeing that he had sketched beautiful and detailed portraits. By some 'other sense', he knew their identities and to whom they were meant to be given. In every case, they were subsequently recognised as deceased relatives by their recipients.

John then felt impelled to set up an art studio in his home where he began to produce, again entranced, oil paintings. These were apparently actually created – and signed – by Pietro Perugino, the 15th century Italian Renaissance Master.

In the studio, I watched in complete astonishment as he painted the beautiful portrait of my 'spirit guide', a Franciscan monk. John was in trance, with eyes closed throughout and muttering in Italian, as paint and brushes flew around at speed; the entire process took just ten minutes. This painting, and a separate pencil sketch of another guide, have remained very special to me ever since.

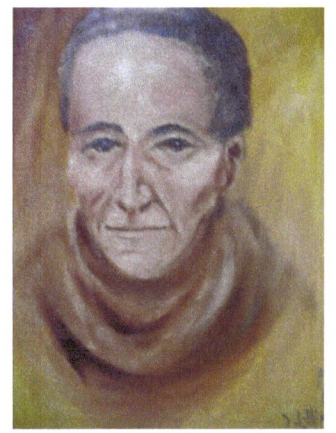

The Franciscan Guide

Thus I was immediately interested when Ann approached me with her fifteen years of research into these phenomena. What I could never have imagined is that, we realised later, she had taught in a school a couple of miles from where I grew up and now lives just a few minutes' walk from the house where I first experienced spirit art all those years ago.

This work has come home!

BIBLIOGRAPHY

Adams, L S	The Methodologies of Art: An Introduction (Westview Press, 2010)
Bangs, M E	The Bangs Sisters' Manifesto to the World (Privately Printed, Chicago, 1909)
Barbanell, M	This is Spiritualism (The Spiritual Truth Press, 2001)
Barrie, D (ed)	Modern Painters: John Ruskin (Andre Deutsch Ltd, 1989)
Beckett, Sr W	The Story of Painting: The Essential Guide to the History of Western Art (Dorling Kindersley, 1994)
Besant, A & Leadbeater, C W	Thought Forms: Illustrated Edition (Dodo Press, 1901)
Bland, T A	In the Celestial World (T A Bland & Co, 1905)
Boddington, H	University of Spiritualism (reprinted by Psychic Press Ltd, 2002)
Buescher, J B	The Remarkable Life of John Murray Spear: Agitator for the Spirit Land (University of Notre Dame Press, 2006)
Burd, v A	Lady Mount Temple and the Spiritualists: An Episode in Broadlands History (Brentham Press, 1982)
Byrne, G	Russell (Janus Pub Co, 1994)
Cheroux, C & Fischer, A	The Perfect Medium: Photography and the Occult (Yale University Press, 2004)
Cherry, D	Painting Women: Victorian Women Artists (Routledge Inc, 1985)
Choucha, N	Surrealism and the Occult (Destiny Books, 1992)

Colbert, C Haunted Visions: Spiritualism and American Art (University of Pennsylvania Press, 2011)

Corlett, A Art of the Invisible (E F Peterson and Son, 1977)

Davies, A J B Portraits from Spirit (AuthorHouse UK, 2011)

Davis, A J The Magic Staff: An Autobiography of Andrew Jackson Davis (reprinted by lulu.com, 2017))

Doyle, A C The History of Spiritualism (The Spiritual Truth Press, 1989)

Dunicliff, J The Traveller on the Hill-Top: Mary Howitt (reprinted by Churnet Valley Books, 1998)

Dvorak, M The History of Art as the History of Ideas (Routledge & Keegan Paul, 1984)

Fenton, J School of Genius (Salamander Press Ltd, 2006)

Fischer A & Oursler T Shannon Taggart: Séance (Fulgur Press, 2019)

Fontana, D Is There an Afterlife? (O Books, 2005)

Garroutte, E M When Scientists Saw Ghosts and Why They Stopped: American Spiritualism in History, in Wuthnow, E (ed) Vocabularies of Public Life (Routledge, 1992)

Gombrich, E H The Story of Art (Phaidon Press Ltd, 1966)

Hayward Gallery Beyond Reason: Art and Psychosis, Works from the Prinzhorn Collection (Hayward Gallery, 1996)

Harvey, J Photography and Spirit (Reaktion Books, 2007)

Houghton, G Evenings at Home in Spiritual Séance: Welded Together by a Species of Autobiography (reprinted by Kessinger Publishing, 2008)

Howitt, A M Pioneers of the Spiritual Reformation: Biographical Sketches (reprinted by Cambridge University Press, 2011)

Jung, C G	Mandala Symbolism (Princeton University Press, 1973)
Kandinsky, W	Concerning the Spiritual in Art (Dover Pub Inc, 1977)
Laine, J-E	The Art of Being Psychic: The Power to Free the Artist Within (O Books, 2006)
Lang, M H	Designing Utopia: John Ruskin's Urban Vision for Britain and America (Black Rose Books, 1999)
Leadbetter, C W	Man Visible and Invisible (Theosophical Pub House of America, 1987)
Levine, P	Victorian Feminism 1850-1900 (Hutchinson Education, 1987)
Manning, M	The Link: Extraordinary Gifts of a Teenage Psychic (Colin Smythe Ltd, 1974)
Miller, P	Faces of the Living Dead: The Amazing Psychic Art of Frank Leah (reprinted by Saturday Night Press Pubs, 2010)
Myers, F W H	Human Personality and its Survival of Bodily Death (new edition Cambridge University Press, 2011)
Nagy, R	Precipitated Spirit Paintings (Galde Press Inc, 2006)
Nagy, R	Slate Writing: Invisible Intelligence (Galde Press Inc, 2012)
Newall, C	Victorian Watercolours (Phaidon Press Ltd, 1992)
Notzing, B v S	Phenomena of Materialism (reprinted by Wildhern Press, 2008)
Oberter, R	Spiritualism and the Visual Imagination in Victorian Britain (Yale University, 2007)
Oppenheim, J	The Other World: Spiritualism and Psychical Research in England 1850-1914 (Cambridge University Press, 1985)
Otto, R	The Idea of the Holy (Oxford University Press, 1972)

Owen, A	The Darkened Room: Women, Power and Spiritualism in Late Victorian England (Virago Press, 1989)
Owen, J J	Psychography: Marvellous Manifestations of Psychic Power Given Through the Mediumship of Fred P Evans (reprinted by HardPress Pub)
Podmore, F	Modern Spiritualism: A History and a Criticism (Methuen & Co, 1902)
Polge, C & Hunter K	Living Images: The Story of a Psychic Artist (reprinted by Regency Press, 1997)
Promey, S M	Spiritual Spectacles: Vision and Image in Mid-Nineteenth Century Shakerism (Indiana University Press, 1993)
Ranciere, J	The Future of the Image (Verso, 2009)
Read, H	A Concise History of Modern Painting (Thames and Hudson Ltd, 1974)
Rothko, M	The Artist's Reality: Philosophies of Art (Yale University Press, 2006)
Russell, C	Groundwaters: A Century of Art by Self-Taught and Outsider Artists (Prestel, 2011)
Saleire	Embracing the Unknown (Sarah Tracy, 2013)
Schapiro, M	Theory and Philosophy of Art: Style, Artist and Society (George Braziller Inc, 1994)
Spiritualists' National Union	Philosophy of Spiritualism (SNU, 2007)
Strode, D	How I Became a Psychic Artist (Athena Press, 2007)
Stuttle, A	The Psychic Artist: Are You Ready for the Challenge? (Self-published, 2007)
Stuttle, A	The Spirit Artist (Farthings Press, 2015)

Swann, I	The Bangs Sisters and Their Precipitated Spirit Portraits (Hett Memorial Art Gallery and Museum, Camp Chesterfield, 1969)
Swedenborg, E	Heaven and Hell (Swedenborg Soc, 1966)
Usborne Moore, W	Glimpses of the Next State: The Education of an Agnostic (reprinted by White Crow Books, 2011)
Wilkinson, W M	Spirit Drawings: A Personal Narrative (reprinted by Trieste Publishing, 2018)

Exhibition Catalogues

Corlett, A	Art of the Invisible: An Exhibition of Psychic Art (Bede Gallery, Jarrow, 1977)
Fraquelli, S	Chagall: Modern Master (Tate Enterprises Ltd, 2013)
Grant, S, Larson, L B, Wright, B	Georgiana Houghton: Spirit Drawings (Courtauld Gallery, London, 2016)
Newall, C	John Ruskin: Artist & Observer (Scottish National Portrait Gallery, 2014)
Pratt, S & Troccoli, J C	George Caitlin: American Indian Portraits (National Portrait Gallery, London, 2013)
Tate Britain	William Blake (Tate Britain, London, 2001)
University of Manchester	Blake's Shadow: William Blake and his Artistic Legacy (Whitworth Art Gallery, 2008)
Zentrum Paul Klee	Paul Klee: The Angels (Zentrum Paul Klee, Bern, 2014)

IF YOU HAVE ENJOYED THIS BOOK...

Local Legend is committed to publishing the very best spiritual writing, both fiction and non-fiction. You might also enjoy:

THE QUIRKY MEDIUM
Alison Wynne-Ryder (ISBN 978-1-907203-47-3)

Alison is the co-host of the TV show *Rescue Mediums*, in which she puts herself in real danger to free homes of lost and often malicious spirits. Yet she is a most reluctant medium, afraid of ghosts! This is her amazing and often very funny autobiography, taking us backstage of the television production as well as describing how she came to discover the psychic gifts that have brought her an international following.

Winner of the Silver Medal in the national Wishing Shelf Book Awards.

AURA CHILD
A I Kaymen (ISBN 978-1-907203-71-8)

One of the most astonishing books ever written, telling the true story of a genuine Indigo child. Genevieve grew up in a normal London family but from an early age realised that she had very special spiritual and psychic gifts. She saw the energy fields around living things, read people's thoughts and even found herself slipping through time and able to converse with the spirits of those who had lived in her neighbourhood. This is an uplifting and inspiring book for what it tells us about the nature of our minds.

5P1R1T R3V3L4T10N5
Nigel Peace (ISBN 978-1-907203-14-5)

With descriptions of more than a hundred proven prophetic dreams and many more everyday synchronicities, the author shows us that, without doubt, we can know the future and that everyone can receive genuine spiritual guidance for our lives' challenges. World-renowned biologist Dr Rupert Sheldrake has endorsed this book as "…vivid and fascinating… pioneering research…"

A national runner-up in The People's Book Prize awards.

POWER FOR GOOD
David J Serlin (ISBN 978-1-910027-31-8)

When we say "Yes!" to the subtle invitations of Spirit, we may find ourselves on exciting journeys of discovery and learning, drawing to ourselves a universal Power for Good that changes us forever. David describes how a chance encounter – and an open mind – led to almost incredible psychic experiences and revelations of spiritual teachings that took him and his wife Linda on a whole new path and new careers. He tells their story here and sets out, in down-to-earth language and with humour, the principles for a happy and fulfilled life.

DAY TRIPS TO HEAVEN
T J Hobbs (ISBN 978-1-907203-99-2)

The author's debut novel is a brilliant description of life in the spiritual worlds and of the guidance available to all of us on Earth as we struggle to be the best we can. Ethan is learning to be a spirit guide but having a hard time of it, with too many questions and too much self-doubt. But he has potential, so is given a special dispensation to bring a few deserving souls for a preview of the afterlife, to help them with crucial decisions they have to make in their lives. The book is full of gentle humour, compassion and spiritual knowledge, and it asks important questions of us all.

SIMPLY SPIRITUAL
Jacqui Rogers (ISBN 978-1-907203-75-6)

The 'spookies' started contacting Jacqui when she was a child and never gave up until, at last, she developed her psychic talents and became the successful international medium she is now. This is a powerful and moving account of her difficult life and her triumph over adversity, with many great stories of her spiritual readings.

A Finalist in The People's Book Prize national awards.

A SINGLE PETAL
Oliver Eade (ISBN 978-1-907203-42-8)

Winner of the national Local Legend Spiritual Writing Competition, this page-turner is a novel of murder, politics and passion set in ancient China. Yet its themes of loyalty, commitment and deep personal love are every bit as relevant for us today as they were in past times. The author is an expert on Chinese culture and history, and his debut adult novel deserves to become a classic.

CELESTIAL AMBULANCE
Ann Matkins (ISBN 978-1-907203-45-9)

A brave and delightful comedy novel. Having died of cancer, Ben wakes up in the afterlife looking forward to a good rest, only to find that everyone is expected to get a job! He becomes the driver of an ambulance (with a mind of her own), rescuing the spirits of others who have died suddenly and delivering them safely home. This book is as thought-provoking as it is entertaining.

TAP ONCE FOR YES
Jacquie Parton (ISBN 978-1-907203-62-6)

This extraordinary book offers powerful evidence of human survival after death. When Jacquie's son Andrew suddenly committed suicide, she was devastated. But she was determined to find out whether his spirit lived on, and began to receive incredible yet undeniable messages from him on her mobile 'phone… Several others also then described deliberate attempts at spirit contact. This is a story of astonishing love and courage, as Jacquie fought her own grief and others' doubts in order to prove to the world that her son still lives.

A MESSAGE FROM SOURCE
Grace Gabriella Puskas (ISBN 978-1-910027-00-4)

Beautiful and inspiring poetry of the Spirit that reaches deep within the consciousness, awakening the reader to higher states of awareness, spiritual connection and love. The author, in familiar and thoughtful language, explores the power of meditation, the nature of the universe and of time, our place within the environment and who we truly are as creative beings of light and sound.

Winner of the Local Legend
national Spiritual Writing Competition.

THE HOUSE OF BEING
Peter Walker (ISBN 978-1-910027-26-4)

Acutely observed verse by a master of his craft, showing us the mind, the body and the soul of what it is to be human in this glorious natural world. A linguist and a priest, the author takes us deep beneath the surface of life and writes with sensitivity, compassion and, often, with searing wit and self-deprecation. This is a collection the reader will return to again and again.

A winner of our national Spiritual Writing Competition.

Our titles are available as paperbacks and eBooks.
Further details and extracts of these and many
other beautiful books may be seen at

www.local-legend.co.uk

www.ingramcontent.com/pod-product-compliance
Lightning Source LLC
Chambersburg PA
CBHW041947240526
45473CB00036B/2405